More Praise for Right Relationship

"Bearing witness to a right relationship between people and nature, Brown and Garver provide better advice for an ecologically sustainable and socially just economy than all the Nobel laureates in economics combined."

> —Richard B. Norgaard, Professor of Energy and Resources, University of California, Berkeley

"This book deserves to sell a million copies. The questions asked—and answered—in *Right Relationship* make a vastly more important contribution to our future than analytical models for maximizing GDP."

> —Herman Daly, Professor, School of Public Policy, University of Maryland, and winner of the 1996 Right Livelihood Award

"The need for radical new ideas, not just reform, to reconstitute the existing economic system has never been more urgent. This monumental book makes a compelling case for the 'right' relationship between human activity and the natural world as the basis for the kind of model that is essential to put us on the pathway to a secure and sustainable future. It is imperative reading for all policy makers and the people on whose participation and support they depend."

> —Maurice Strong, former Under Secretary-Gen   nd
> Special Advisor to the Secretary-General of th
> Nations

"Out of the rich Quaker tradition of personal cc
peace, equality, and justice comes this powerf
our relationship to the earth and its commc   ec-
ognizing the inherent connections betwee   , social well-being, and a moral economy, t   vided,
for Quakers and non-Quakers alike, lig   .ess."

> —Curt Meine, conservationist and au   .o Leopold:
> *His Life and Work*

"Right Relationship offers up a welcome and needed change to the technocratic and ethically empty programs that have dominated the sustainability challenge. At the same time the book grounds its arguments in practical terms that can be enacted into new forms of governance and social behavior."

> —John R. Ehrenfeld, Executive Director, International Society for Industrial Ecology, and author of *Sustainability by Design*

"The challenge mankind faces of turning around our planetary emergency will require a revolution as enormous as the agricultural revolution ten thousand years ago. Our only chance for effecting this transformation in the basic ways we do business with the planet is for a critical mass of the population to 'get it.' *Right Relationship* lays out the case as comprehensively and compellingly as any work on the subject that has come to my attention."

> —Alex Shoumatoff, Contributing Editor, *Vanity Fair*, and author/editor of DispatchesFromTheVanishingWorld.com

"This book looks at the root causes of our accelerating ecological problems. It should be read by politicians, business leaders, the public, and above all our youth. It is they who have to face the consequences of past actions. Reading this book, I hope they will unite and speak with one voice for economic and institutional change to create a right relationship between humans and our planet."

> —Helen R. Hughes, first Parliamentary Commissioner for the Environment, New Zealand

"*Right Relationship* is the right book at the right time. It is a compass directing us toward a life-centered economy that reflects our highest values."

> —David Orr, Paul Sears Distinguished Professor of Environmental Studies and Politics, Oberlin College

"*Right Relationship* is absolutely right: we need to redesign our economic system so that our relationship to life trumps our relationship to profit. Peter Brown and his colleagues show us how this can be done. Everyone who wants a better world should read this book."

> —Peter Barnes, author of *Capitalism 3.0*

"To reclaim modern economics from the gospel of infinite growth and an idolatry of the market is to be reminded of the wisdom of Aquinas who noted that what is required for genuine happiness is sufficiency of material goods and virtuous action. This book provides an important road map for virtuous action in building a new civilization of love and an economy of well-being built on the pillars of the four virtues of western civilization, which Plato defined as courage, moderation, justice, and wisdom."

> —Mark Anielski, author of *The Economics of Happiness: Building Genuine Wealth*; CEO, Anielski Management; and Adjunct Professor, University of Alberta School of Business

"In 1942 Aldo Leopold wrote, 'Our whole cultural structure is built of non-durable materials which will sag as the land weakens.' This persuasive and compelling book elaborates on this theme: a weakened and sagging land. But it offers us hope with an innovative framework for change—a new story. Brown and Garver envision a global community, a whole earth economy with a new kind of grounding and understanding, bringing science and ethics together."

> —Nina Leopold Bradley, Director, The Aldo Leopold Foundation

"This book is a blessing. Basing their ideas on the fundamentals of the way the earth actually works, Brown and Garver lead us on pathways of respect toward a mutual flourishing of humans and nature. We humans can elect an abundant future rather than devouring the livelihood of our grandchildren as current economics demand."

> —Paul Heltne, Director, Center for Humans and Nature

"This is a book for our times. It offers a blueprint for the way forward out of the ecological and economic upheavals wreaked by the relentless pursuit of economic expansion. As we consider the prospect for humanity's ability to avoid catastrophic change to earth's life support-systems and achieve economic and social stability, the authors' proposals for a new global governance framework, including a global reserve, are spot on."

> —Janine Ferretti, Chief of Environment Division, Inter-American Development Bank, and former Executive Director, North American Commiss'ion for Environmental Cooperation

"A just, resilient, and secure future for the earth and its habitants will require a shift in human values and a sense of shared responsibility for finding ways to live within ecological limits. *Right Relationship* provides clear analysis and provocative solutions that should resonate with all who seek an economy that reverses course from its current dangerous trajectory."

> —Adam Koniuszewski, Chief Operating Officer, Green Cross International

"How is the international community going to solve the dilemma of relying on economic growth as the answer to poverty in the world, even though it is clear that ecological pressures due to unlimited growth are already severe and accelerating? *Right Relationship* provides a thoughtful set of options for creating an economy built on new answers to this pressing problem."

> —Sheila Abed, Chair, International Union for the Conservation of Nature Commission on Environmental Law, and founder and Executive Director, Paraguayan Environmental Law and Economics Institute

Right Relationship
Building a Whole Earth Economy

PETER G. BROWN

GEOFFREY GARVER

WITH KEITH HELMUTH

ROBERT HOWELL

STEVE SZEGHI

Berrett–Koehler Publishers, Inc.
San Francisco
a BK Currents book

Berrett-Koehler Publishers, Inc.
235 Montgomery Street, Suite 650
San Francisco, CA 94104-2916
Tel: (415) 288-0260   Fax: (415) 362-2512 www.bkconnection.com

Ordering Information
Quantity sales. Special discounts are available on quantity purchases by corporations, associations, and others. For details, contact the "Special Sales Department" at the Berrett-Koehler address above.
Individual sales. Berrett-Koehler publications are available through most bookstores. They can also be ordered directly from Berrett-Koehler: Tel: (800) 929-2929; Fax: (802) 864-7626; www.bkconnection.com
Orders for college textbook/course adoption use. Please contact Berrett-Koehler: Tel: (800) 929-2929; Fax: (802) 864-7626.
Orders by U.S. trade bookstores and wholesalers. Please contact Ingram Publisher Services, Tel: (800) 509-4887; Fax: (800) 838-1149; E-mail: customer.service@ingrampublisher services.com; or visit www.ingrampublisherservices.com/Ordering for details about electronic ordering.

Berrett-Koehler and the BK logo are registered trademarks of Berrett-Koehler Publishers, Inc.

Printed in Canada
Berrett-Koehler books are printed on long-lasting acid-free paper. When it is available, we choose paper that has been manufactured by environmentally responsible processes. These may include using trees grown in sustainable forests, incorporating recycled paper, minimizing chlorine in bleaching, or recycling the energy produced at the paper mill.

Library of Congress Cataloging-in-Publication Data
Cataloging data is available from the Library of Congress.

ISBN 978-1-57675-762-8

First Edition
14 13 12 11 10 09   10 9 8 7 6 5 4 3 2 1

Cover & Interior Design: Mayapriya Long/Bookwrights   *Copy Editor:* Mark Woodworth
Proofreader: Henrietta Bensussen   *Indexer:* Medea Minnich
Production Service: Linda Jupiter Productions

To Suzanne Moore

Contents

Foreword
Thomas E. Lovejoy

IT IS NO SECRET that the state of the global environment is extremely worrisome and getting worse literally daily. The world is headed for massive impairment of natural systems and soaring extinction rates, with global biogeochemistry already seriously out of balance. This is so despite many efforts to safeguard and restore the environment. Indeed, working on the environmental agenda can seem tantamount to running up a down escalator.

So if ever there was a time to consider the right relationship of humanity and the environment, both in the general sense of the phrase as well as in the important sense of the Quaker tradition, it is now. This book could not be timelier.

The heart of the problem, in many senses, lies at the intersection of economics and ecology. Both words, as has been often pointed out, come from the same root, namely the Greek *œcos*, meaning *house*. Yet despite the best efforts of some very good economists and ecologists the two disciplines remain far apart without even a common vocabulary, and this lack of integration is a major factor in the downward spiral of the global environment.

One problem is the way neoclassical economics attempts to bridge the gap by recognizing externalities, namely those things not accurately reflected in market prices. For example, important efforts such as work on the pricing of environmental goods and services, gets us away from the idea that nature is free for the taking. That probably was fine for our australopithecine ancestors, but with our swelling population and prowess at commandeering resources the end is already in sight. It is not possible for the current population to live a developed world lifestyle, nor is it possible for all of us to live as hunter-gatherers. We will need to be more creative than simply getting all the prices right in fitting the economy to a finite planet. In this quest, prices surely have a role to play. A practical example is the market created to reduce the contribution to acid rain by the sulfur in power plant emissions. Current discussions about raising the price of carbon are headed in a similar direction by giving us incentives to live within the earth's biophysical limits.

A second obstacle is the concept of substitution, that is, when one resource is exhausted it can be replaced by another, as whale oil was replaced by fossil fuels. As biologists, we know by definition that one species can never completely substitute for another, even when their roles in ecosystems might be fairly similar. Even if two had identical roles, one is not expendable; our own bodies tell us that redundancy has value, which is why, for example, we have two kidneys. Would we want to have an ecosystem or planet with the equivalent of a single vital organ?

A third great challenge is the application of discount rates that basically make it easier to put off addressing problems unless their immediate costs to humanity are so great as to warrant up-front expenditure. Interestingly, Sir Nicholas Stern decided not to apply discount rates in his economic analysis of the challenge of climate change, because otherwise society's response would be too little, too late.

If, as has been pointed out, the economy is the wholly owned subsidiary of the biosphere, there needs to be a way for human action and the economy to transcend the obstacles and move humanity toward a sustainable, respectful course.

First, we need to recognize that we benefit both directly and indirectly from the environment and in ways complex and hard to measure. Huge and regular benefits will frequently accrue to humanity through advances in the life sciences from new insights based on what was previously an esoteric organism. Human societies value knowledge and libraries, but we have yet to transfer that approach to the enormously valuable living library of the life sciences represented by the diversity of life on earth. Until we do, soaring extinction rates make book burning, and the attendant ignorance, look pale in comparison.

Second, we need to think carefully about what we mean by "growth." I have often wondered about possible lessons embedded in ecology that could be of use in developing more-sustainable economies. Biological systems have two forms of growth. In the more obvious one, the organism simply gets bigger through consuming more resources; sometimes that ceases at adulthood, but in others, like alligators, with indeterminate growth, the organism simply grows larger until it reaches the end of its life. In the second, known as growth by intussusception, the organism does not grow larger but becomes more complex. Although the analogies in economic growth may rarely be so distinct, surely the information industry has a large element of complexity, as contrasted to natural resource use.

Clearly the time is at hand—indeed, it is overdue—for a grand reconciliation between humans, human systems, and the environment. This very solid and thoughtful book sets the stage for just that, and we all are much indebted to the authors and those who labored in the Moral Economy Project.

Only a call to our higher values and their integration into our socioeconomic system can achieve what is needed. That may seem like a vainly grand ambition, but in many senses we have no other choice.

Belief in a higher being is widespread in human societies. There could be no higher calling than to recognize that our incredible living planet and humanity's future are inextricably intertwined. I cannot but believe that as a species able to produce soaring achievements in the arts and science we have the capability to achieve right relationship.

Preface

THE WAY THAT PEOPLE provide for themselves is in growing conflict with the integrity of Earth's ecological and social systems. The disconnect is so severe that it is now easier to imagine Earth's life-support systems breaking down than to imagine that our ecologically incoherent and destructive economic system will be significantly altered.

Our concern about this lethal failure of imagination drove us to write this book to bring focus and direction to the growing, urgent cries for change. Our purpose is to offer people from all walks of life an ethical guidance system based on "right relationship." This book aims to integrate scientific understanding with an ethical stance and spiritual optimism informed by that understanding. This integration of ethics and science grounds an innovative governance for the well-being of Earth's entire community of life. We hope that a new orientation built on these foundations, and on humanity's enduring ethical and cultural traditions, will help people to organize their individual and collective economic lives in a way that promotes a flourishing community of life on Earth.

Most of us have been conditioned to accept the operation of today's global economic system as an article of faith. We have learned to view unlimited growth and wealth accumulation as the "natural law" of the economy, and we were taught that nothing can be done to alter this fact—even if it means the integrity of Earth's ecological and social systems will be severely damaged or even permanently compromised. This "inconvenient truth" poses a moral challenge. While this is not explicitly a Quaker book, its use of right relationship as a point of focus arises from the same deep commitment to human solidarity, human betterment, and the well-being of the commonwealth of life that the Religious Society of Friends (known as Quakers), as well as many others, endeavor to carry forward and put into practice in the world. We hope the idea of right relationship as a way to build a whole earth economy resonates with people from a broad range of life experience as they wrestle with the moral challenge posed by a lethal economy.

This is not the first time that moral challenge has confronted the growth-driven economy. We found inspiration for this book in heartening stories of our Quaker forebears. On the afternoon of May 22, 1787, a group of twelve men met in a Quaker bookstore and printing shop at 2 George Yard in London. This meeting of nine members of the Religious Society of Friends (Quakers) and three Anglicans was the start of a catalytic campaign for social change. This small group was determined to end British participation in the slave trade and abolish slavery throughout the British Empire. They were deeply convinced that slavery was a wrong relationship between humans, and the need to put it right impelled them to take action.

Quakers, along with many other citizens who shared their vision of right relationship in both England and America, had already taken a stand on slavery and had been working to arouse the conscience of their respective nations against an economy based on it. Their general opposition had had little effect, because "everyone knew" that slavery was ordained by "natural law" and essential to the economic growth of the Empire.

The organized campaign of moral suasion that Quakers and their Anglican allies launched from that meeting in the printing shop successfully challenged the "natural law" of slavery and its economic status. In 1791, a report to Parliament by a Select Committee on the Abolition of the Slave Trade still characterized the slave trade as having "the plea of necessity for its continuance." Yet the next year Parliament passed its first law banning the slave trade.

Fast-forward two centuries. In June 2003, thirty-nine Quakers met at Pendle Hill, a Quaker study center in Wallingford, Pennsylvania, to consider the moral challenge posed by the global economic system that is heedlessly destroying the integrity of Earth's ecosystems and failing to serve the well-being of hundreds of millions of people. The gathering included economists, ecologists, and public-policy professionals determined to look deeply into the conflict between economic trends and ecology, with a view to understanding the full moral context of our deteriorating human–Earth relationship.

The participants did not feel daunted. They came well prepared, and together they advanced a larger moral context for economic analysis and for reconceptualizing the economy within a vision of ecological stewardship and the well-being of the entire commonwealth of life. Soon after, the Quaker Institute for the Future (QIF) was born as a venue for research, joining a community of other Quaker organizations, such as Quaker Earthcare Witness in the United States, the Quaker Environmental Action Network in Canada, and Quaker Peace and Social Welfare in Great Britain, as well as non-Quaker groups worldwide too numerous to mention with similar concerns. QIF initiated the Moral Economy Project, from which this book comes, as its first avenue of witness and service.

Those eighteenth-century Quakers and their allies who launched the movement to end the slave trade, and slavery itself, eventually won the day and brought down the economic interests that argued for the "natural law" of profit over all. We are inspired not just by that singular victory, but also by the work of several other Quakers who took action to promote changes based on their deep conviction that something was not right. One of them, John Bellers, a British Quaker who lived in the late seventeenth century, was the first social thinker to conceive of universal health care as a public policy. He was the first economist to advance a comprehensive plan for vocational training and sustainable employment as a national solution to chronic poverty.

Another person who had immense impact on history was John Woolman, an eighteenth-century American Quaker, who traveled widely to speak out against such social ills as slavery, greed, and material excess. He even insisted on paying the slaves of the people he visited for their service on his behalf. Largely as the result of his efforts, slave-holding among American Quakers ended a full century before the Civil War. A third was Lucretia Mott, an American Quaker who was an antislavery crusader and women's rights leader; along with Elizabeth Cady Stanton, she organized the 1848 Seneca Falls Convention, the first American women's rights meeting. Closer to our own time was Bayard Rustin, an African-American Quaker, who was a leading behind-the-scenes strategist of the nonviolent movement for civil rights in twentieth-century America. British Quaker business entrepreneurs in the eighteenth and nineteenth centuries, such as the Lloyds, the Cadburys, the Rowntrees, and the Quakers who founded Friends Provident (the first pension and ethical fund), showed by example that business activity and investment can be both profitable and principled.

The ecological perspective that has increasingly come to be part of the spiritual life of Quakers has roots in their history that are as deep as their social concerns. John Woolman, for one, clearly understood that unwise use of resources leads to ecosystem breakdown, in the same ways that unjust use of labor leads to societal breakdown. In 1763, he visited two Native American villages in what is now northeastern Pennsylvania. He noted in his *Journal* the way that Native peoples had been driven from the resource-rich lands and waters of the coastal regions into the rougher, more difficult lands of the interior. He lamented the greed and drive for wealth accumulation that robbed Native peoples of their land and livelihood. He wrote that the land under English tenure was rapidly being depleted of its fertility by the growing of large quantities of grain for export to Europe, while the poor laborers and their livestock were suffering for lack of adequate and affordable forage.

Woolman clearly saw "the spreading of a wrong spirit," and wrote that "the seeds of great calamity and desolation are sown and growing fast on this continent." He urged his fellow countrymen, according to what he called "universal righteousness" (in effect, right relationship), to "rise up . . . and labour to check the growth of these seeds that they may not ripen to the ruin of our posterity."[1]

When Woolman kept his *Journal*, the calamity had already happened for Native Peoples; the American Civil War was yet to come. And now the seeds of the economic, ecological, and social calamity that Woolman understood would reach far into the future have sprouted into a massively invasive set of wrong relationships. The ruin he feared is today clearly seen in the breakdown of life-support systems unfolding worldwide.

John Woolman is a key inspiration for the establishment of the Quaker Institute for the Future, the Moral Economy Project, and even the writing of this book. Kenneth Boulding, a twentieth-century American Quaker, an economist, and a pioneer in general systems analysis, is another. He was among the first social scientists to recognize Earth's ecological context as the primary reference for all progressive thinking, policy, and action with regard to the human future. In 1965 he gave a short address to Washington State University's Committee on Space Sciences, the title of which introduced a powerful metaphor—"Earth as a Space Ship." A year later he wrote and published an expanded essay on this seminal image—"The Economics of the Coming Spaceship Earth." Boulding's work in this and many other essays and studies is exemplary of the integrative, holistic approach that has helped to create the ecological worldview and establish this new way of understanding the human–Earth relationship.[2]

Boulding was fully conversant with the cosmological and earth sciences that structure our ecological worldview. He was especially skilled in laying out the implications for human economic behavior, based on what we now know about how "spaceship Earth" functions. In his later years, he initiated a seminar program that he called Quaker Studies on Human Betterment. As with John Woolman, this book, along with the Quaker Institute for the Future and the Moral Economy Project, grew directly from the legacy of Kenneth Boulding.

In a profound sense, economics and ecology are domains of relationship. Economics is about access to the means of life. Ecology is about the mutual interdependence of life communities. Using right relationship as the unifying mechanism, this book brings these two perspectives together, pivoting the lens of human solidarity and the lens of ecological science into a single focus. Right relationship becomes the central motif both in the social design of human well-being and in ecologically sound economic adaptation. The Quaker tradition teaches that in right relationship, people may touch the fullness of human meaning, and, some would say, the presence of the Divine. Quaker practice is about elevating all areas of human policy and practice into this zone of right relationship.

This book, written by a cooperative group, emerged from the Quaker tradition of dialogue and truth-seeking. The Moral Economy Project and the authors of this book start with the fact that human well-being is entirely dependent on the well-being of the whole commonwealth of life.

The Introduction gets things started with definitions of key terms, such as "right relationship," "commonwealth of life," and "whole earth economy." Although a number of moral terms are possible candidates for inclusion in a definition of "right relationship," we have chosen to ground it, with some modification, in Aldo Leopold's land ethic, set out in his seminal book *A Sand County Almanac.*

Then we introduce five questions that are discussed in detail in the book's five chapters: *What is the economy for? How does it work? How big should it be? What is a fair distribution of its benefits and burdens? How should it be governed?* Right relationship is the key to answering these questions in a way that will allow the economy to nourish and preserve the community of life on earth, instead of working toward its destruction. Using right relationship as the guide leads to some surprising answers. The economy exists for respecting and preserving life, not getting rich. Its frame of reference must be the laws that govern the cosmos as well as the earth—not just, for example, the laws of supply and demand. The economy can grow too big for the earth's ecological limits, which means that endless growth is an irrational goal. Fair distribution of the economy's benefits and burdens means it is possible to be both too rich and too poor. Governing a whole earth economy will require a new set of rules and institutions that have the support of the entire global community and that invigorate local communities and innovation, rather than stifle them. Answers to the five questions forge a way for people to work together to build a whole earth economy, step by step.

Economics based on consumerism and obsession with growth has become, in effect, the modern world's state-sponsored religion. This economy now needs, for the sake of the human future and indeed the future of the entire community of life, the same wind of change that was earlier directed at abolishing the economy of slavery. Nobody who aspires to human solidarity and ecological integrity should rely on the political-financial establishment and its supporting cast of economists and policy makers even to envision these changes, let alone bring them about. With the guidance system set out in this book, we are endeavoring to link hands with all those now rising up to build a whole earth economy—one that restores and enhances the integrity, resilience, and beauty of life's commonwealth.

Peter G. Brown
Geoffrey Garver
Keith Helmuth
Robert Howell
Leonard Joy
Steve Szeghi

September 2008

Introduction
Moving from Wrong to Right Relationship

"BEARING WITNESS" IS THE Quaker term for living life in a way that reflects fundamental truths. Bearing witness is about getting relationships right. The group of Quakers in the eighteenth century who built a movement to end slavery were bearing witness to the truth that slavery was wrong. Yet bearing witness to right relationships is not limited to Quakers. It is something done by inspired people of all faiths and cultures when they live life according to cherished values built on caring for other people and being stewards of the earth's gifts. The mass movement to end apartheid in South Africa, Rachel Carson's triggering of the environmental movement in the 1960s, and the campaign of Mothers Against Drunk Driving to make roads safer are just a few examples of people coming together to bear witness to what they knew was right.

The global economy today is overwhelming the ability of the earth to maintain life's abundance. We are getting something terribly wrong. At this critical time in history, we need to reorient ourselves in how we relate to each other and to the earth's wonders through the economy. We need a new mass movement that bears witness to a right way of living on our finite, life-giving planet.

Right Relationship

Over just the last two decades, science has radically altered its view of the arrangement both of life and of nonliving components of the earth. New understandings are emerging that place relationship at the center. Biology and physics are moving away from a "reductionist" view of function, in which the activity of a living cell or an ecosystem, for example, is explained by being reduced to its parts, rather than including the relationship between those parts as essential to our understanding. Today scientists are admitting that this three-hundred-year-old scientific doctrine is far too simplistic, and are finding that physical substances work and exist in terms of highly complex, interdependent, and changeable *contexts* and *relationships*. So, for example, the relationships between genes in the human body, rather than only their individual functions, are the key to the countless ways that human genes can produce genetic traits and characteristics. We are now learning that relationship is the key to the survival of our species on the social and political level, as well. This book, then, is about relationship writ large, and about how to move to right relationship from wrong relationship in our individual and collective economic lives.

A quick story of one set of relationships operating on our planet helps illustrate this more sophisticated scientific understanding. In its natural state, oil, created over eons from organic matter by volcanic heat and compression, is found almost entirely within the earth's crust; that is its *natural relationship* with the planet. By the same token, most forms of life can only exist within the biosphere; the thin membrane of plants, animals, and microorganisms and their life support systems at or near the earth's surface constitutes habitat for virtually all life. Life on earth also exists in a *spatial relationship* to the atmosphere, which must contain gases also arranged in a particular relationship—not too much carbon dioxide, plenty of nitrogen and oxygen, only minute amounts of other gases. Finally, all life forms need access to a highly particular relationship between only two simple and very plentiful gases: hydrogen and oxygen. Water, so necessary to life, is in fact a relationship between those two gases. It is also found primarily on top of the earth's crust or only a short distance beneath it or in the atmosphere above it.

These relationships can equally easily be discerned to be "wrong" if the spatial configuration of each component is seriously disturbed, just as a gene sequence cannot express itself if it does not have the necessary position in the genome and the necessary relationship with certain proteins.

Right now, one of the largest industrial projects in the planet's history is located in western Canada. Development of the Alberta tar sands is a massive attempt to alter the relationships of the substances normally found below the earth with those on it. In this case, oil is brought from beneath the crust along with the sand it permeates and placed in relationship to the ecosystems found on the surface: forests, rivers, wetlands, and lakes. Once on the surface, the oil enters into a relatively permanent set of new relationships with air and water, both in Alberta where it is mined, and also when it is used in vehicles and heating plants in the chain of refineries and users that spread out from it, as far west as China and as far south as Texas. The immense Athabaska River, adapted over millennia and nourishing the boreal forest, enters into a long-term new set of relationships, too. To flush oil from the sands, the river is drained, boiled, forced through the oil-drenched sands, and then deposited in enormous tailing ponds, where the oil's poisonous hydrocarbons are supposed to "settle." The life-giving water of the Athabaska is removed from any use by life forms ever again, barring the discovery of some new, extraordinary technology.

This alteration of relationships transforms the thousands of square miles devoted to tar sands development into a huge, toxic graveyard of former life, with a stench of sulfur and hot asphalt that can be smelled from far away. The surface of the earth is stripped of all animal or plant habitat. In the surrounding area, pus-filled boils, cancers, and other lethal diseases and birth defects in the fish, animal, and human population are now being documented.[1] But not only are ecological relationships affected. Tar sands development also affects social relationships among people. Tens of thousands of workers have migrated to the few towns and many work camps on the site. The crime rate in the towns and cities most affected, Fort McMurray and Fort Chipewayan, and Edmonton and Calgary, has risen, as have homelessness, the cost of living, and prostitution. Human casualties from drug use, alcohol, highway accidents, and the rigors of shift work on a frontier are also escalating.

And these are only the impacts at the beginning of the chain. Once shipped from Alberta, tar sands oil will power air conditioners in deserts, furnaces in the Arctic, and many cars, trucks, and jets. It will serve as the raw material for a vast array of synthetic chemicals and fertilizers. This single industrial project even affects Canada's international relationships, as it makes the nation's compliance with emissions reductions in the Kyoto Protocol virtually impossible. Demand for Alberta's oil will be driven by an international economy that is racing ahead in pursuit of endless growth and wealth accumulation.

Alberta tar sands development, along with many other modern industrial developments such as the Three Gorges dam in China or even the war in Iraq, are clear examples of "wrong relationship."

In this book we expand the term "right relationship" from its early Quaker use to give it a more universal meaning that includes contemporary science and has roots in diverse cultural and religious traditions. Right relationship provides a guiding ethic for people wishing to lead fulfilling lives as creative and integrated participants in human society and the commonwealth of life as a whole. It is akin to what some would call "sustainability," though it goes much deeper. Right relationship offers a guidance system for functioning in harmony with scientific reality and enduring ethical traditions.

In the 1940s, conservation biologist Aldo Leopold, reflecting on what he had come to see as the next stage in human moral development, created a useful definition of right relationship. When working out what he called the land ethic, he explained that "A thing is right when it tends to preserve the integrity, stability, and beauty of the biotic community. It is wrong when it tends otherwise."[2] Many volumes have since been written on the philosophy of ecology, but this simple statement has become the touchstone of the ecological worldview. Leopold's ethic gains strength when enhanced with affirmations of the inherent value of human and other life, as exemplified in Albert Schweitzer's powerful idea of "reverence for life."[3]

Replacing the term "stability" with "resilience" reflects the current scientific understanding of relationships. Leopold's ethic applies, as well, to the integrity, resilience, and beauty of human communities. How the ethic is understood in practice depends, of course, on the type of community. Hence, with only one alteration, his ethic becomes a practical guide for differentiating between right and wrong relationship both in human society and in the entire community of life of which humans are a part: "A thing is right when it tends to preserve the integrity, resilience, and beauty of the commonwealth of life. It is wrong when it tends otherwise."

It is quite possible to choose right relationships and the common good. Many individuals are already doing so, as are many communities and a few societies. The problem the world is currently facing, however, is that in most of our modern societies the majority

A thing is right when it tends to preserve the integrity, resilience, and beauty of the commonwealth of life. It is wrong when it tends otherwise.

of people are actively urged, even forced, to choose wrong relationships, such as those typified by the Alberta tar sands project. Greed and the constant stimulation of new desires that feed it, until quite recently regarded in most societies as sinful or at least unpleasant, have increasingly become acceptable, even glorified. Simultaneously, modern industrial activity has embraced a pathological gigantism, increasing corporate consolidations and ruthlessly crushing the small-business players, as well as the natural systems on which all economic activity depends.

In short, a pursuit of wrong relationships is the prevailing trend of our times. The signs are now well known: climate change, over-population, loss of topsoil and fresh water, increasing rates of species extinction, deforestation, imperiled coral reefs, unstoppable invasive species, toxic chemicals that remain for eons in the environment, persistent human poverty and hunger, and an increasingly inflated, unstable world financial system and globalizing economy. And we only begin the list.

Right relationship with life and the world is both a personal and a collective choice, but it is a choice that we must make. It can support and inspire people struggling to find a foundational base for the development of productive societies and a healthy human–earth relationship. Opting for healthy human and ecological communities is a decision we can make that will require us to find new ways to live and to run our economies. Of course, "right relationship" is simply another way of expressing similar precepts found in many of the world's religious and spiritual traditions. The reductionist science of the eighteenth and nineteenth centuries transformed ethical ideas by removing, for many people, their theological foundations. Now, the relationship science of the late twentieth and twenty-first centuries is beginning to change human perceptions of reality, particularly in terms of human duties to the other life forms with which we share life's prospect.

The Commonwealth of Life

To move from wrong to right relationship, we need to answer the question: related to what? To answer this question we have chosen a term that stresses interdependence—commonwealth. It is typically used to describe a political community established to promote the *common* good, rather than only the interests of individuals or a particular class of people. Political commonwealths derive from the roots of the word: "common" and "wealth"—that is, wealth is seen as something to be allocated equitably in society, to be shared in common.

The traditional idea of a commonwealth stresses the shared features of the community and interdependence of its members. For people, relationships with other humans or with natural communities bring in notions of mutual respect and fairness that are reflected, for example, in universally recognized moral principles like the Golden Rule. The commonwealth of life extends these notions of common features, fair sharing, and interdependence to the entire community of living beings on the earth. The "common wealth" in this community of life on the earth is now clearly the evolutionary heritage and destiny that people share with other life forms. A whole earth economy works for *all* of life's commonwealth. Hence the subtitle of this book.

Nearly all life on the earth has been made possible by the power of the sun, which over eons has fueled the creation of living structures of increasing complexity and interdependence. These range from single-cell organisms to elephant, honeybee, or human societies, as well as the intertwined communities of plants, animals, insects, and other biota that constitute a forest. In the commonwealth of all life, the actions of each individual member or species affect the entire commonwealth, however small the result might be. We human beings are now in a position to have far greater impact on the commonwealth of life than most of the other life forms with which we share the planet. Therefore we have the responsibility and privilege to consider other beings and ecosystems when we engage in any sort of social action, including an economy. Our actions must embody an ethic of appreciating, husbanding, and sharing the earth's bounty.

An Economy in Right Relationship

Our species has arrived at its present precarious condition through a history of development driven, in part, by economic relationships and interactions. But though it has facilitated convenience in material living over the centuries, building and maintaining human societies has often had disastrous effects on human and natural communities—the ruin of the Mayan, Roman, and Easter Island civilizations are examples. By objective measures, the kind of globalized economy that has seized the world since World War II is one of the most disastrous of all. Many of the earth's key life-support systems are in rapid decline.[4] Far more catastrophic collapses are likely to hit human and ecological communities in the near future, and the long-run prospect is dire indeed unless a shift from wrong to right relationships becomes part of human culture.

The postwar financial success of a globalized economy has led to the continuing expansion of finance and consumption and to prosperity for hundreds of millions of people, but it has also trapped the nations of the world in a relentless pursuit of economic growth with no thermostat or shutoff valve. Especially since the end of the Cold War and the easing of any threat of a competing ideology, an increasingly unregulated global capitalistic economy, as developed most enthusiastically in the United States, has dismantled decades-old institutions and structures that had previously succeeded at more evenly distributing prosperity and reducing market abuses.[5]

The current system operates on the assumption that the earth's environment is a subset of the human economy, and that the earth belongs to humans. If these are the assumptions, it makes sense to transfer as much of the earth's natural capital as possible into the engines of the industrial economy. These assumptions, though, are fantastically at odds with scientific reality; human culture and its economic goals are, in pure scientific fact, a subset of the earth's environment and resources, and humanity is only one of millions of species that depend on them. Like putting water into the tar sands, placing the human economy above the well-being of the natural world creates a lethal, poisonous wrong relationship. So how can people shift from an economy based on greed and unquestioned growth to a whole earth economy that is based on right relationship with the commonwealth of life?

Five Questions in Search of Right Relationship

Five key questions, and their answers, chart a path to putting the economy in right relationship with life's commonwealth:

- What is the economy for?
- How does it work?
- How big is too big?
- What is fair?
- How should it be governed?

The balance of this introduction offers an analysis of each question, with a summary of the "wrong relationship" problem to be solved and a preview of answers based on right relationship.

Question #1: What is the economy for?

What are people aiming for, individually and collectively, in the myriad interdependent transactions that make up the economy? Most leaders in finance, business, government, and think tanks say that the global economy's purpose is to enhance human well-being by constantly maintaining economic growth. They assume, despite having little or no serious argument or data, that more consumption and economic activity will result in greater well-being.

Yet this answer makes no sense. To begin with, in mainstream economic terms, growth is not measured in terms of benefits, but simply keeps track of overall economic activity in terms of exchanges of money. Many such exchanges create negative side effects, such as pollution, but money spent on cleaning up the resulting pollution is measured as positive growth—and hence adds to dominant measures like Gross Domestic Product (GDP). So, for example, the current economic model sees the money spent cleaning up the Exxon Valdez oil spill as an increase in GDP and therefore beneficial. Similarly, when a person suffers a fatal car accident, the economic exchanges, in terms of ambulances, insurance agents, funeral homes, and so forth, increase GDP and are seen as positive.

The current purpose of the economy—providing ever-increasing wealth, with ever-increasing growth—means that cash incomes can rise while actual wealth falls, as measured by natural capital such as soil, timber, oil reserves, and clean water. Making money often demands the one-time, windfall liquidation of centuries-old natural support systems such as forests or fisheries, or even older works of nature such as the Canadian tar sands.

In addition, GDP growth contains no measure of *distribution*, so inequity, poverty, and outright starvation often can, and do, rise at the same time that overall economic activity increases.

Lastly, many studies worldwide have demonstrated that after certain basic needs are met, it is one's relative wealth—how folks compare to others, not an absolute amount of wealth accumulation—that determines much of the self-perception of happiness. In "advanced" (or, perhaps, "overdeveloped") societies, trying to improve well-being and happiness through growth is folly on a treadmill, since people cannot all be wealthier than each other.

These problems are symptoms of an economy in wrong relationship. Right relationship, by contrast, is built, in large part, on respect for all life—the kind of respect that is inherent in the Golden Rule, fair play, and other ethical principles that people from across the world's religions and cultures learn as children. Once the economy is understood as being embedded in the living, dynamic world that surrounds it, its purposes become clear: that is, to maintain the integrity, resilience, and beauty of life's commonwealth. The human economy is our way of provisioning ourselves. Hence for humans this means providing for the well-being of individual people, households, communities, and nations. It also means providing for the health and vitality of the finite ecological community in which we live—our diverse and finite earth. Moving away from an economy based on wrong relationships does not spell economic doom. Rather, it creates opportunities for truly rich and fulfilling lives for all.

Question #2: How does the economy work?

The prevailing way of thinking about how the economy works is to imagine that the economy is the box in which social interactions, ecosystems, and their resources are contained. The current economic order has a wrong relationship with how the real economy of this planet works. First, it assumes that the earth is subsidiary to the economy. Second, it mistakes a measure of wealth—money—for wealth itself. Third, it does not know how to think intelligently about the by-products of economic activity that are not the desired outputs—what we typically call waste.

How Does the Earth Work?　In a typical mainstream economics textbook, the economy is represented by a circular flow diagram. It depicts the production and consumption of goods and services without regard to the components of the earth or life's commonwealth needed to produce them. In fact, about a century ago economists stopped considering any concern for the adequacy of such resources as food and energy. Mainstream economics today proceeds, with rare exception, with no reference to the laws of physics, chemistry, or biology.

To understand how a human economy actually functions, it must be conceived of as being embedded in, and also a major determinant of, the complex systems whose relationships make up the earth's ecosphere.[6] This requires a basic scientific understanding of how the planet works, which in turn requires some understanding of how the universe itself works. Kenneth Boulding, an economist and pioneer of complex systems, pointed out in the 1960s that the earth can be thought of as a spaceship: The material available for economic activity is limited to what is already on board the craft floating in the universe.

The fact that the earth is a system closed to matter has important implications. For all practical purposes, nothing ever enters or leaves. But the earth is open to energy. It receives a continuous flow of energy from outside the system in the form of sunlight, and it radiates roughly the same amount of heat back into space. This flow of heat from the sun is a key factor in making life on the earth not only possible, but abundant. The energy from past sunlight is stored in coal, oil, and natural gas. These are called *stocks*. Present and future sunlight is called *flows*.[7] Both stocks and flows of sunlight are finite, and this inescapable fact places limits on the earth's life-support capacity. Understanding this fact forms an essential foundation for building an economy in right relationship with life and our earth.

What Is Wealth? Everything on the earth gives us our wealth. We typically treat wealth as solely a matter of money. In fact, money is a human tool exchanged for the real things that make up wealth: edible plants and animals, useful objects such as containers or furniture, the land and soil that can continue to produce real wealth in the future. Valuing the symbolic value (money) higher than the real one has led to the wholesale neglect of what makes this wealth possible.

The fundamental wealth on the earth, on which all else depends, is the ability to maintain life itself, which is made possible by the ability of green plants to convert sunlight into sugars. Plant-based sugars are wealth. They are used by the plants themselves and by virtually all other organisms to sustain themselves and to reproduce. Without this simple activity, all the manufactured capital, all the human capital, all the social capital, all the money, all the bank deposits, and all the credit cards on the earth—the totality of these not only would be worthless, they would not exist. An economy in right relationship with real wealth is built on the simple fact that the integrity, resilience, and beauty of natural and social communities depends on the earth's vibrant but finite life-support capacity.

The fundamental wealth on the earth is the ability to maintain life itself.

What Is Waste? Like symbolic wealth, waste does not exist in nature. All materials—from cow dung to lava flows—are reused or recycled for a huge variety of purposes. On the surface of the planet, nature's "wastes" support all life. Within conventional economics, the undesired products of an economic activity are viewed as useless "waste." If they are not priced, they are viewed as external to the market. This is what is called the "theory of externalities." The basic idea is that the prices paid in a transaction often do not include all the costs of production. For example, without some kind of correction, the $50 paid for a tire will not reflect the damage done to the lungs and laundry of people who live downwind of the plant where the tire is made. Because this unintended by-product is considered "external" to the market, it is a cost that the tire manufacturer and the consumer never pay, in an unregulated market.

Making the tire manufacturer pay for the pollution and harm it causes is an example of the "polluter pays" principle, which is extremely appealing at first glance. If you are going to cause harms, then you should pay for them. Even so, the polluter-pays principle is not an adequate solution to the pollution, toxic substance, and "waste" stream problem.

First, it is often impossible to calculate the monetary costs of pollution. How much harm will any given amount of additional carbon dioxide in the atmosphere—which speeds up global warming—cause by changing monsoon patterns in India over the next century?

Second, while the polluter-pays principle, in theory, allows a business or institution to pollute as much as it wishes as long as it is willing to pay for the pollution, there are some things that should be prohibited, rather than tolerated as long as compensation is paid. No amount of compensation will make up for a child killed or deformed by toxic chemicals in her playground.

Third, the polluter-pays principle is almost always applied in an anthropocentric way, assuming that only costs to humans matter. A deformed and dying frog population is regarded as irrelevant unless people are also affected.

The theory of externalities also fails to consider that, strictly speaking, there is no such thing as a "by-product." All results of manufacturing and processing industries are direct products, whether they are useful or not.[8] In a whole earth economy there is no such place as "away," as in "throw it away." All worn-out or cast-off products remain within the ecosystem. All economic activity is internal to the biosphere.

To fashion an economy existing in right relationship with life's commonwealth, a big jump is needed to an entirely different conceptual framework and accounting system. Only an economy that completely outgrows the idea of "waste" can work on spaceship earth, where all products of manufacturing and other processes must be accounted for. In a whole earth economy, materials internalization would replace cost internalization: Manufacturers would be responsible for recycling as much energy and material as possible. Similarly, the notion of consumption, which implies an ending or discarding of the material consumed, must give way to a notion of *transformation* of the material into the beginning of something else. This is what is called the "waste is food" or "cradle to cradle" approach.[9] In a whole earth economy, refusal to tolerate *any* waste has to become the goal for all economic activity.

The European Union is taking important steps in this direction. Today every car or washing machine coming off the assembly line in the EU must be recyclable. All the components must either be recycled by the earth (if benign) or reused in the industrial stream (if poisonous), thereby using the nonabsorbable heavy metals and petrochemicals again to make more machines. Legislation to this effect has been in effect for years in Germany, for example, though it still seems light-years away to North Americans. Of course, during the operation of an appliance like a washing machine, soap, bleach, and other by-products will be used and discarded—which also must be processed by the earth's systems.

Question #3: How big is too big?

How does the earth's finiteness affect how we think about the economy? Pondering this focuses attention on the issue of whether the economy could be too big, too fast, or too intense. The current economy has no measure of "enough." It has no means of saying when growth has become what economist Herman Daly has termed "uneconomic"—when the negative effects of growth outweigh the benefits.[10] An economy in right relationship with the planet has a thermostat, complete with a shutoff valve, that prevents economic growth from shutting down the very life-support systems on which the economy depends.

Understanding the question of scale starts with the fact that plants are the basic energy source from which all animals (including humans and their cultural projects) ultimately come. Plants get their energy from sunlight. The global growth economy is overly dependent on consuming sunlight from the past that is stored in fossil fuels. It shifts many of the ecological consequences of current economic activity to the future, building up carbon dioxide in the atmosphere and taking heavy metals from under the earth's surface and scattering them throughout the surface environment.

We humans can do the math; we *know* that renewable resources such as soil, forests, and fish are now being consumed at a rate faster than they can be replenished, and we know that greenhouse gases are increasing dangerously in the atmosphere. Most of us recognize that this simply does not work over the long term. An economy without a thermostat or shutoff valve—for example, having no way to make drastic cuts in greenhouse gas emissions despite an overwhelming scientific consensus that indicates not doing so will lead to catastrophic climate change—is in wrong relationship with the commonwealth of life. This means that we are still not effectively answering a simple question: How big should the economy be?

The economy's growth and size, as well as its intensity, velocity, and momentum, must be judged at every turn by its impact on the "integrity, resilience, and beauty" of human society and ecological communities. The *momentum* of the economy is especially important to keep in mind. For example, because so many impacts of human economic activity are growing on such a massive scale, even if greenhouse gas emissions were to start decreasing immediately, and even if emissions were to equal nature's withdrawals, it would still take decades, even centuries, for the climate to stabilize.

Measuring the scale of the economy and its impacts on social and ecological communities will require rigorous scientific inquiry and monitoring of indicators of both ecosystem and social-system health and resilience, on a global scale. In today's economy, scientific research tends to favor profit-making pursuits. Tracking the scale of the economy will take a much greater commitment to scientific research aimed at the common good—at developing a comprehensive understanding of how key life-support systems function. New measures of societal and ecological well-being, many of which already have been proposed, will need to be refined and then substituted for current measures of economic growth—GDP, in particular.

A method of doing all these things is derived from the I=f(PATE) framework, based on work by Paul Ehrlich and John Holdren.[11] This framework says that the human impact on the global ecosystem (*I*) is a function (*f*) of the complex interplay among population (*P*), affluence (*A*), technology (*T*), and ethics (*E*). Understanding this set of relationships provides a means for figuring out how to keep the human economy within the earth's ecological limits.

Question #4: What's fair?

In laying out his "spaceship earth" metaphor, Boulding pointed out that "we have a two-deck spaceship": one deck for the haves and one for the have-nots.[12] Yet the current economic order has no measure of fairness. Its main antidote to poverty is more growth— justified by the facile slogan that "a rising tide lifts all ships." In many countries and regions of the world, notably China and India, growth has indeed been a major factor in moving hundreds of millions out of poverty. But in the four decades since Boulding wrote, the human population has approximately doubled. It is a sad fact that those people in the world today who are desperately poor still number in the hundreds of millions.[13] At this point in history, we can no longer afford to try to address poverty through aggregate growth. To do so is simply unfair to future generations of humans and other species.

Determining what is fair also must take into account the enormous current and future ecological harm ranging from soil erosion and species extinction to massive destabilization of climate through greenhouse gas emissions. Hence, Boulding's vision needs to be expanded. We tend to think only about how humans should be sharing the benefits and burdens of living with *other humans*. An economy in right relationship has to include the fair sharing of the earth's life-support capacities with all of life's commonwealth. In a whole earth economy, fairness requires that we seek a flourishing earth—a world that works for all.

Question #5: How should the economy be governed?

Throughout history, humans have cooperated to establish rules that all members of a community or society are expected to follow. Even the most fervent supporters of the free market would concede that some rules are necessary. The question, then, is: what rules? How are they established and enforced? Which rules characterize our institutions today?

Under the leadership of the thirty countries of the Organisation of Economic Co-operation and Development (OECD), money and its surrogates have become more and more detached from government regulation and control. The world economic powers insist on "free trade," minimally regulated by national or international authorities. They also work to ensure that capital investment and financial markets remain minimally regulated by any publicly responsible body. This global free-for-all puts mounting pressure on social and ecological communities, which are wrongly assumed to be adequately protected as long as global GDP continues to climb. Governments are increasingly answerable not to their electorates, but rather to the financial interests that help politicians attain positions of authority and spend vast resources to influence governance decisions.

Unfortunately, many of the current piecemeal government solutions to the combination of problems threatening the global commons often exacerbate the problem. Examples such as genetically engineering crops to increase food yields, or using biofuels to provide a renewable source of fuel, will almost certainly increase ecological and social problems. Both require enormous monocultures, machinery driven by and fertilizers derived from fossil fuels, and the use of industrial patents, which affects land use and tenure and entails huge wealth-distribution problems, as well as genetic and chemical pollution. The fundamental reason the solutions are often even more dangerous than what they replace is that they grow out of and perpetuate the insane drive of industry and government for limitless growth. They often still serve wrong relationships.

What kind of governance is required for a whole earth economy? Current international institutions lack adequate mechanisms to understand, let alone manage, the ecological limits that place limits on the economy's size; to protect global commons; to establish global ecological rules that all the world's nations and citizens must live by; and to ensure that those rules are obeyed. For this reason, new and more effective governance is urgently needed at the global level. The missing global governance functions could be established in various ways. Four global institutions can be envisioned that would put them in place: an earth reserve; some form of global federalism; global environmental trusteeships; and a mandatory world court.

A *Global Reserve* would gather and analyze information on the ecological impact of the human economy. Key elements of such information would be research, monitoring, and analysis needed to assess the economy's scale limits, allocation, and distribution. This information, built around refined indicators of the health and resilience of social and ecological communities, would also serve the other global institutions.

A *Global Federation*, admittedly, can seem repulsive at first glance. Yet people seldom recognize that the entire planet is already under global governance of a nondemocratic and destructive kind that undercuts life's prospects. For example, most countries have already subjected themselves to the authority of the World Trade Organization and the International Monetary Fund, which often impose disastrous choices on formerly independent and self-sufficient countries and localities. Currently, the most effective transnational institution, in terms of how it protects ecosystems and human cultures, is the European Union, though it must be disentangled from the current economic paradigm, and the ecological impact of the average European is still too high.[14] It differs from other international governance organizations in that it is more democratic and relatively transparent. The new Global Federation could be modeled, in part, on the EU and given jurisdiction over the operation of a whole earth economy, but with important decentralization features that maintain local control and innovation as much as possible. This is the crucial principle of subsidiarity. One of the Global Federation's primary duties would be to design policies to ensure a fair way to share access to life's basic necessities.

Trusteeships of Earth's Commons would protect the ozone layer, the atmosphere, the oceans, and the other global commons necessary for life's flourishing, by monitoring and administering the limits and allocations deemed necessary through the work of the Global Reserve.

Finally, a *Global Court* would resolve disputes arising out of the operation of these institutions and hold them to their charters.

Such institutions as these might seem hopelessly idealistic. But what is truly unrealistic is the idea that continuing down the current economic path will ever serve the common good, or save the life forms and cultural traditions of this planet from their march toward extinction.

Four Steps to Achieving a Whole Earth Economy

Study after study has shown that reaching the goal for which we humans have placed our entire planet at risk—economic escalation and personal wealth—does not even make us happy. Above a certain amount needed to maintain a roof over their family and put food on the table each day, human beings in every country surveyed are not made happier by more material goods, even in significant amounts. What *does* make us happy are the ideals promoted by almost every ethical tradition known: belonging to a community; enjoying good health; sharing; loving and being loved; having access to nature; making a meaningful contribution. When we envision the true limitations, responsibilities, and mystery of living on the earth, we will begin to experience far more fulfilling lives than the excessive acquisition of material possessions can ever provide.

What can be done, then, to start building a whole earth economy in right relationship with life's commonwealth? The first step on this new path is *grounding and clarification*. Right relationship is based on feeling a sense of awe for the cosmos and embracing an ethic of humankind's appropriate place in, and relationship to, the cosmos and the earth. Grounding and clarification begin with the recognition that it makes much more sense to be inspired to live within the ecological limits of the earth than to ignore the ecological consequences of relentless economic growth. People everywhere need to envision having fulfilling lives, and then start living them by walking more lightly on the earth. Plenty of books, Internet resources, and community-based organizations provide creative ways to do this. With first grounding and then clarification, a whole earth economy can start to take hold.

Second, building a whole earth economy will require *development of models, pilot programs, and techniques* based on right relationship, informed by history but tailored as best they can be to the future. The global institutions envisioned in this book require further discussion and development; perhaps other approaches will better provide the governance functions urgently needed at the global level. Whatever institutions emerge must preserve local decision making, yet ensure respect for new, ecologically based rules that we all must live by to avoid the further unraveling of life's commonwealth and the attendant decline in the human prospect. This is not something that should only be left to "experts." What will daily life be like when a new kind of global governance comes into play? The answer will depend not only on the details of how global governance functions, but also on how it makes sense in the daily lives of people in communities across the globe. The more people who participate in discussing new forms of global governance, the better it will serve people and the entire commonwealth of life fairly and effectively.

The third step is *bearing witness to a guidance system built on right relationship*. As a better future built on right relationship comes into sharper focus, a mass epiphany is bound to take place. Everyone who wants to preserve the integrity, resilience, and beauty of the commonwealth of life for future generations needs to commit to individual and collective changes that will lead to right relationship. It is impossible to predict how or when this epiphany will take place. But it *is* possible to hope for it and work for it by bearing active witness to the concept of right relationship and to the urgent need for change.

The last and catalytic step in this vision for building a whole earth economy is *the igniting of a social movement of nonviolent action* that changes hearts, minds, and policy toward right relationship. Quaker history contains many stirring examples of action leading to the advancement of significant social and economic reform, while the Quaker template for abolishing both the slave trade and slavery itself against powerful, entrenched interests is the most well known. The Quaker example can serve as an inspiring model for building a whole earth economy in right relationship with life's commonwealth.

1

What's the Economy For? A Flourishing Commonwealth of Life

Today the main object of business activity is to make a quick profit, the quicker the better. The main object of contemporary statecraft is to make societies ever richer. To what end, and with what effect on individual and social virtue, we no longer ask, and scarcely dare think about. Keynes was the last great economist to hold economics in some sort of relation to the "good life." But already the language available to him to talk about the relationship sounded threadbare. What, in fact, was the connection between being rich and being good? Keynes was troubled by such questions but could make little progress in answering them. It became sufficient to keep the existing system of wealth creation going, because its collapse would be more horrible than its success.

— Robert Skidelsky[1]

TO CONSIDER WHAT THE purpose of the economy is, it may help to begin with a small snapshot of an economy working in right relationship.

When members of the community of Woodstock, New Brunswick, organized the Woodstock Farm Market in the 1970s, they made a few rules: local producers selling their own produce only, and no produce from wholesalers allowed. Right off, however, the organizers had to make some exceptions that seemed fair and consistent with the spirit of the market. For example, if your neighbor had extra strawberries, it was okay to put them on your table as a favor. And they would allow one particular vendor who brought fresh fish from the Bay of Fundy to set up a table, as the townspeople really wanted fresh seafood, and what he brought was as "local" as seafood was going to get.

Baked goods, jams, jellies, and pickles had to be homemade. Craft items had to be locally made, as well. The emphasis on local production was not only a matter of providing opportunity for local growers, but an effort to help build an ecologically sound local food system. Many growers who sold at the market ran small-scale, environmentally respectful operations. In many cases, vendors favored organic methods. The market also served as an information exchange network on sustainable practices for local conditions.

Sometimes, "local" got stretched pretty far if the product was not already offered by an area vendor. For example, a family from the next county brought in lawn furniture made from native white cedar. A vendor of ready-to-eat foods came from a considerable distance; his German sausages were a big hit. The market manager constantly had to work with the board of directors to make decisions on what fit within the guidelines and what made sense for the organization's development.

The founders wanted their market to be a place for direct selling by the producers. When peddlers who didn't meet the criteria asked for space, the Woodstock Market had to refuse them, and explain why. Sometimes they would set up just outside the market to take advantage of the crowd, and then the market manager had to confront them with an argument about purpose and fairness. Sometimes they refused to leave. The town backed up their farm market managers in these instances, and before long the word got around. Most people respected what the market was trying to do and found the rules reasonable.

Then the Woodstock Farm Market ran into pricing issues. Each vendor was free to set the prices for produce offered. But the members said, let's be fair about it. When various crops come in, let's check with each other on what we consider a fair price and pretty much stick with it. It does make sense to set different prices for differences in quality, and maybe do a little markdown or make bulk deals at the end of the day. But beyond that, if we try to outcompete each other we all lose. We will informally school new vendors in our ways of market pricing.

Occasionally someone set a price that undercut the rest, especially when tomatoes came in. The manager talked it over with the price-cutter and usually got cooperation or maybe a compromise. If not, word spread, and the price-cutter soon found the market to be a rather uncomfortable place to do business. Some didn't care, but then they usually didn't last long. Members eventually came to know each other and wanted everyone to sell enough to make it worth coming back. So they cooperated.

The story of the Woodstock Farm Market is the story of an economic market. But it is also the story of how the purpose of that little market economy grew from the community and folded back into it. That is a market that is embedded in the norms of the community and sees that community in its ecological context.

Simple questions often have unexpectedly complex answers. "What is the purpose of the economy?" is such a question. Getting the purpose of the economy right is important. It enables people to orient their engagement in the economy. When, as individuals, we buy things, invest our money, or barter and trade, or when as a community—local, national, or international—we adopt the rules and policies that govern the economy, that's the time to ask ourselves whether we are helping to achieve the economy's purpose, and, especially, what that purpose is.

At first blush, in light of conventional wisdom, the economy's purpose may seem to be obvious: to provide ever-increasing wealth through unlimited economic growth. If we work toward this purpose, we are told, then society, community, and the environment will all be well-served. Borrowing from the future and creating huge debt loads to ensure economic growth is no problem, because growth will ensure the ability to repay the debt—whether in rich countries like the United States or developing countries selling off their resources in return for international loans. According to this mainstream economic analysis, community issues like health and education, as well as care of the environment, can only be addressed by wealthy societies; so the first priority is always to concentrate on that economic growth. This is an answer grounded in *wrong* relationship.

Right relationship leads to a very different answer to the question "what is the purpose of the economy?" Isn't it reasonable to think that the purpose would focus on the well-being of communities and the individuals who make them up? In a whole earth economy, the purpose of the economy is to preserve and enhance the integrity, resilience, and beauty of the whole commonwealth of life. A whole earth economy is not necessarily a no-growth economy. It is an economy with other priorities: providing rich and fulfilling lives for both individuals and communities, but without pushing toward extreme wealth and advantages that destroy social and ecological well-being. The Woodstock Farm Market, as well as the many markets and community cooperatives like it, has the flavor of right relationship.

A whole earth economy provides rich, fulfilling lives for individuals and communities.

Where Did "The Economy" Come From?

To see why the economy needs to orient toward a new purpose, it helps to remember where the concept "the economy" came from.[2] The economy, as it is now understood, began relatively recently. Before the eighteenth century, farmers, tradesmen, craftsmen, and other businesspeople sold, traded, and bartered their goods and services within well-defined social contexts. Economic activity took place within the social order and as part of social life. That economy was closely tied to the fluctuations of the local environment and climate. The Woodstock Farm Market would have felt right at home in the eighteenth century.

During the course of that century, the economy broke away more and more from its ties to communities, the local environment, and the social order. Land ownership became a more powerful basis for asserting economic might, industry and manufacturing began to take off as a result of technical innovation, a larger and increasingly wealthy elite started accumulating enormous financial power, and long-distance trade expanded significantly. Although banks have existed for thousands of years, the era of modern banking began only in the late eighteenth century. Money and all its baggage—borrowing, interest, credit, speculation—took on a more central role in providing the means of life. More and more, society and the environment became subservient to wealth accumulation and expansion of the economy.

Out of this transformation arose the idea of the self-regulating market. Such a market is assumed to take care of the negative side effects of the economy and to work for the common good all by itself. Belief in a self-regulating economy became a significant factor in the disruption and reconfiguration of social and ecological relationships during the Industrial Revolution. The market economy that began its modern expansion in the nineteenth century undercut relationships and concerns that did not feed into its growth and financial power. The increasingly influential brokers of the market economy lobbied government officials with the message that the market was the true and best engine of progress, and that it was therefore fitting for the market to have power and control over the entire range of social and ecological relationships. As the market economy arose, the artificial entity called the corporation arose, as well, and over time the corporate duty to maximize shareholder profits increasingly has overridden the accountability of corporations to society.

By the end of the nineteenth century, belief in the moral supremacy of the market reached a peak, especially in North America. Social Darwinism was the prevailing philosophy: The people with the most money and power were seen to reflect a perfectly normal and acceptable form of "survival of the fittest." This was the heyday of monopolies and union-busting, of the robber barons, John D. Rockefeller's empire at Standard Oil, and the like—what is called "laissez-faire capitalism," with all its excesses and social upheavals that led to the founding of labor unions and the strengthening of Socialist movements.

At various times and places, societies rebelling against laissez-faire capitalism have demanded regulation to protect people, communities, social institutions, and the environment from the market's harsh brutality. Labor laws that created minimum wages, restricted working hours, prohibited child labor, and protected the right to unionize stemmed the concentration of power and money of the robber barons of the early twentieth century in the United States. Antitrust laws did their part, too. Social security, socialized health care, and environmental protection laws also arose eventually to place limits on market forces. Almost miraculously, the wise decisions to create publicly managed national parks and forests and wildlife reserves arose in the United States around the same time that the great monopolies of the Gilded Age were peaking in the early 1900s. Yet, then and now, the push for an unregulated market has remained a strong current in the global economy, especially in the United States and other wealthy countries.

The notion that economic growth was a crucial social and political necessity gradually took hold, particularly in the period following World War II, and explicitly at the start of the Kennedy Administration in the United States in 1961.[3] It has held on ever since. It rested in part on carefully worked out theories that Paul Samuelson synthesized in the 1950s and 1960s and that became the standard of the profession. All the predictions of standard economic theory rest on assumptions, and market failure is what happens when these assumptions turn out to be false—as they nearly always do.[4] Correcting these failures provides a robust role of government. Too robust by far, it seems, for many who stand to gain from the market.[5] Free-market ideology virtually ignores the well-grounded claim in standard theory that government intervention is needed to address market failures.

Yet free-market ideology has regained dominance in the Western world since the early 1980s. Laissez-faire capitalism, or market fundamentalism, is the belief that there is no reasonable alternative to a virtually unregulated market for understanding economic relationships, engaging in productive economic pursuits, and, ultimately, promoting the common good. This, however, is not science, and is not even economics: It is analogous to a religious faith.[6] According to this creed, governments should do nothing other than define property rights and enforce contracts.

The "laws of economics" on which market fundamentalism claims to be based have their origin in the particular set of property and social relationships that were current when Adam Smith and other moral philosophers were studying the economy systematically in the eighteenth century. Not only have market fundamentalists terrifically distorted Smith's analysis of how to run a proper economy, but the "laws" he and other early theorists "discovered" were particular to the political economy of their time. They were not laws encoded in cosmic nature for all time and circumstances. This distinction is important. Understanding that the economy is dependent on circumstances and not governed by contrived "laws of nature" is a liberating insight. It makes people realize that they can choose alternatives, and it makes clear that our current circumstances require a different approach.

In seeking a whole earth economy, the choice is not between market fundamentalism and standard theory—for both are oriented to growth, irrespective of ecological impact, as a primary objective of economic policy.

A saving grace of the economics profession is that some frontline economists have understood this problem and are working out the terms of reference for a steady-state or negative-growth economy that may well be needed to provide for long-term ecological and social well-being.[7] The first great step toward building a whole earth economy is to unlock the mental straitjacket that market fundamentalism and its public-policy advocates have decreed to be the only rational way to think about the purpose of the human economy. Within the larger scientific framework of a whole earth economy, many of the insights of standard theory, unlike those of market fundamentalism, find a congenial home.

The Social Heritage of Providing for Human Needs and Desires

Understanding how goods and services were made available to people before the invention of the modern market economy is the easiest way to envision the potential for a whole earth economy. The starting point for building this vision is to acknowledge that the baseline purpose of the economy is to provide access to the means of life, which also means asking the question: What is life all about? Biologists tell us that human nature is built on basic desires to reproduce, to ensure basic security and comfort, to display possessions and wealth as a means of obtaining and keeping mates, and to cooperate and associate with like-minded people.[8]

Of course, there are many ways to express and satisfy those desires. Obviously, humans also engage in complex moral, aesthetic, and religious behaviors. The economy reflects the way that people individually and in community go about providing the means to these activities. What, then, distinguishes the community-oriented economy of the Woodstock Farm Market from the ruthless economy of the pyramid schemer, the oil speculator, or the junk-bond dealer?

The Woodstock Farm Market, like many traditional economies, provides access to the means of life within a context of ecological sensitivity and mutually supporting social behavior. Cooperation in mutually beneficial economic dealings is the ethical root of society. The key elements of this kind of cooperation are respect and reciprocity: respect for other people and for the environment, reciprocity in the form of the give-and-take that leads to mutual satisfaction in the form of fair treatment. From the earliest human societies of nomadic hunting and gathering groups, providing access to the means of life was framed by a code of reciprocity: If you share some of those roots you found, I will give you a cut of the antelope I just brought down. Inequities and conflict certainly occurred. But without an underlying sense of fairness, in which social relations were continually rebalanced, as they are in chimpanzee and many bird societies, our ancestors would not likely have proceeded very far on the great trek of human evolution.

Once farming, the domestication of animals, and the cultivation of storable grains reached a level where some people started having surpluses, the stage was set for those holding the surpluses to claim superiority based on their greater ability to help others survive. Thus, political forms of domination, beginning with early chieftainships, have unfolded across subsequent human history. Wealth accumulation and control of access to the means of life have been the plot for this part of the human story—with claims of special access to the will of God and divine right also playing their role in the history of domination. The varied wielders of power in history have asserted their control, ruling over those with "less" in ways that were sometimes brutal, sometimes beneficent.

Through all those centuries of hierarchical domination, respect and reciprocity never disappeared. These values remain at the heart of all cultural and ethical traditions. They are so encoded in human experience that children get a sense of them at a quite early age. The Golden Rule, the magic of getting more when you share, the innocent rage at being treated unfairly: Children learn early what right treatment by and good relationship with others feels like. To be undercut, these basic values have to be intentionally crushed. And that is exactly what an economy does when it encourages the amassing of wealth and rewards greed, all in the name of more indiscriminate growth. Our present economy tempts us too often to satisfy our basic biological drives—reproducing, security and comfort, display of consumption, and taking sides—by trading in empathy, bonding, and social unity for winning at all costs and climbing the social ladder so as to lord it over others.

The Fundamental Persistence of Respect and Reciprocity

History has stories in which the spirit of respect and reciprocity prevailed, and others telling how cheating, brutality, and violence reigned for long periods. Examples of both still exist today. Since 1972, for example, Bhutan has measured its social well-being in terms of Gross National Happiness—a sign of its decision to promote quality of life over getting rich and raising GDP. In Myanmar, by contrast, a brutal military dictatorship suppresses the people's will and manages the country's wealth for its own purposes. Despite this mixed record, respect and reciprocity have not only endured through history, they have also emerged as ideals to which all cultures of the world aspire—even if, in practice, they are often cast aside. Many international declarations are built on the principles of respect and reciprocity, such as the 1948 Universal Declaration on Human Rights. Likewise, the 1992 Rio Declaration affirms the international community's commitment to sustainable development and to protecting the environment for future generations.

One reason that these principles have endured is that they have deep roots in history. During the time that the German philosopher Karl Jaspers and others identify as the Axial Age,[9] a six-hundred-year period in the first millennium BCE, a series of great religious thinkers and philosophers in world history appeared. Each bore witness to a fulfilling, spiritual way of living that drew on a deep sense of right relationship. These figures include Confucius, Lao-tzu, Siddhartha Gautama (Buddha), Asoka, Isaiah, and Amos (along with other Hebrew prophets); and, later, Jesus and Muhammad. Their teachings and examples all point to a spiritual path to self-worth and meaning more profound and gratifying than the accumulation of wealth, power, and empire that marks so much of human history.

The great thinkers of the Axial Age laid down universal foundations of right relationship that have lived on through the ages. Their messages of compassion, mutual aid, community service, human well-being, and respect for life provide the basis for people of *all* cultural and religious traditions to lead a life respectful of the integrity, resilience, and beauty of the entire commonwealth of life. Some have referred to the Reformation as a second Axial Age, and to our current ecological crises as the opening to another pivotal era of spiritual renewal.[10] Whether it is called a new beginning or a time of regrounding in long-recognized principles, the time is right for a pivot toward an economy in right relationship with the commonwealth of life.

> *The time is right for a pivot toward an economy in right relationship with life's commonwealth.*

The Wisdom and Witness of Indigenous Cultures

Another context of cultural experience must be added to this picture. Indigenous peoples have often remained within the circle of a particular wisdom about human relations and the human–earth relationship, if only because they live in such intimacy with the realities of life and survival on this planet. A heritage of social experience based on respect and reciprocity can be found if one looks for common beliefs within the remaining teachings of the elders of many North American indigenous communities.[11] Still today, many traditional peoples aspire to fairly common ideals and values and follow an ageless code for living in harmony with all the other beings and structures of the earth. This discussion draws primarily on North American indigenous cultures, but is generally congruent with the cultural ways of indigenous peoples in many other regions of the world.

Perhaps no other characteristic illustrates so clearly the common ethical beliefs of indigenous social life as the attitude toward children. Some years ago Jean Briggs, an ethnographer, conducted a study of Inuit child-rearing practices and titled her book *Never in Anger.*[12] One surprising discovery for her, coming from the mainstream nonindigenous culture, was that not only was it completely unthinkable for an adult to strike a child, it was also a rule of relationship never to correct or deal with a child in any way from the unworthy footing of anger. This is not to say anger may not arise, but the disrespect and inequity of thrusting it on a child is considered unacceptable.

This bears witness to one of the key elements of traditional ethical systems passed down through generations—respect. Respect for children, for family, for oneself, and all others; respect for the ancient lineage of grandmothers and grandfathers; respect for all living beings, for the land as a living being, for all the gifts of the land and all the beauty of the earth; respect and continuous gratitude to all spirits, to all the elements of the earth and sky, and to the web of life. Without this circle of respect and gratitude filling the heart and mind, a person stumbles through life from one catastrophe of wrong relationship to another.

This is how the behavior of many Europeans appeared to indigenous peoples in North America. Most Europeans, to the native groups they encountered, seemed bereft of the awareness and intelligence of fully formed humans. Hence, for example, the bewildered horror of the Cree of Northern Quebec to the practices of southern hunters even today, who take a haunch or a trophy head from a caribou but leave the rest of the animal to rot. The lack of respect this shows, both to the animal that had given up its life and to the land that provided it, so shocked the young Cree of Chisasibi that they filmed hours of video to expose this crime through the media— never realizing that to the mainstream media, wasting an animal in this way is not a moral issue.[13] Still today, indigenous peoples must continually push to have their traditional knowledge of how the earth works recognized in the policy arenas where many decisions that affect them are made.

When indigenous peoples of North America began to understand that their use of the land was being stolen permanently, they realized that *respect* as they knew it played no part in most Europeans' intentions for the future, or in their view of relationships. When they witnessed the slaughter of the buffalo, and that great tide of life on which they depended vanished from the plains, their world was unhinged by such monstrous disrespect and deliberate, wasteful destruction.[14] When they witnessed the tall-grass prairie cut into ribbons and literally overturned by the steel plow, they saw a disrespect for the earth that filled them with despair. In those days, the enterprising farmers thinking only about feeding the growth of the capital-driven grain markets back east, like Quebec's hunters today, would have seen this reaction as benighted.

It is now known that in causing vast loss of topsoil, the "plow that broke the plains"[15] was an engine of enormous ecological destruction. Thousands of tons of soil and fertilizer wash into the Gulf of Mexico each year because farmers have wrong relationships with the land of the Plains. The result is a growing dead zone in the Gulf and degraded soil on the Plains that requires even greater use of industrial fertilizers to keep it productive. The mind of respect and the dream of cultural longevity that stands behind ecologically coherent adaptation plays no part in this game of maximizing short-term profit and ignoring long-term loss. Among the many contributions indigenous cultures have made to the human prospect, respect is now being recognized for its survival value in social and economic adaptation. Respect is increasingly in the minds and hearts and on the agenda of all those who are seeking a hopeful way into the future.

An ethic of respect, given at every turn and expected in return, creates the emotional wellspring that is critical for communities living in right relationship with the commonwealth of life. Respect at this level was critical for eons of successful adaptation for our species. It is no less critical for the social and ecological survival of communities, nations, and all peoples in the present. The place of respect in right relationship with life and the world is one of the key moral lessons that indigenous peoples contribute to understanding a whole earth economy.

The Vision of a Whole Earth Economy

A whole earth economy takes no more than it needs and uses no more than it must. Building a whole earth economy means moving from endless production and concentration of wealth to providing only as much wealth as is needed for dignified, secure living. It means moving from the burnout of unlimited growth to the resilience of continuously renewed abundance. A whole earth economy is keyed to the resources of local and regional ecosystems, and to the shared abundance of the earth's ecosystems as a whole. This vision of a whole earth economy does not see a dangerous or restrictive depression of economic activity, but, on the contrary, an intensification and a flourishing of all the productive, provisioning, service, and trading activities that create and support the integrity, resilience, and beauty of life's commonwealth. This, surely, is the purpose of the economy.

2

How Does It Work? Putting the Economy in Its Place

If a living system does not respect the circumstances of the super system it is a part of, it will be selected against.

—Eric Schneider and James Kay

A HAYFIELD WITH MULTIPLE species of grass, scattered blooms of wildflowers, and populations of field mice, voles, and songbirds sets the stage for a story of both economics and ecology: a story of how the economy works. If the hayfield is mowed in timely fashion when rain can be expected, it will regrow and can be cut a second time (in moderate climates) and still achieve additional regrowth before winter. The hayfield's resilience depends on a critical variable, rain, because of the relationship of rain to other variables. Although mowing will affect their numbers, mice, voles, and songbirds will still be present, along with hawks, owls, and foxes that feed on them. The livestock fed by the hay, the farm family fed and supported by the livestock, the farmer's customers and all the wildlife and grasses of the hayfield—all favor this state of affairs.

However, if the hayfield is cut too late or if no rains come, it may become a dusty field of stubble, with coarse invasive plants and saplings rapidly attempting to establish a different system. If things go well, though, eventually another system with its own integrity, resilience, and beauty will emerge. Or if severe erosion, salinization, or desiccation occurs, the field may remain bereft of life, or with only unhealthy communities.

Natural or minimally managed systems on which the economy depends are generally resilient as long as key variables, such as rain in the hayfield, stay within certain limits. Maintaining healthy systems first requires understanding how they work and what their limits are, and then requires care not to exceed those limits. This is a central principle on the path to a working, resilient, and ecologically coherent economy. Thinking about how the economy works only in conventional terms like supply and demand, market dynamics, financial incentives and the like, misses the big picture. The big picture starts with a basic scientific understanding of how the earth life systems on which the economy depends work, which has implications for both religion and ethics, which in turn give rise to a new sense of citizenship in the commonwealth of life. It ends with the realization that a merging of new understandings of science and ethics requires new thinking about key economic terms and about how the economy works.

Setting the Stage for Reframing the Economy

The activities characterized as "the economy" emerged within recent human history. The human species emerged from a long, historical context—that of biological evolution. Biological evolution emerged within the context of photosynthetic, biochemical, and metabolic processes. This complex of processes became established on the earth within the context of geochemical properties bathed in solar energy. The geochemical properties of the earth and its solar environment in turn emerged within the context and history of the universe. This is the heritage of the human economy, and the context from which a coherent understanding of how it works emerges.

The remarkable scientific developments of the last two centuries are almost entirely absent from the framework of contemporary economics. When science is taken into account, it becomes clear that the economy is embedded in human society, which is a subset of the commonwealth of all forms of life in the global ecosystem, which in turn is an island of life in a vast cosmos. In shifting from thinking about what the economy is *for* to thinking about *how it works*, seeing the economy as embedded in the global ecosystem and subject to the laws of the cosmos graphically illustrates how the economy can help preserve and enhance the integrity, resilience, and beauty of the commonwealth of life. Why is this important? The science that underlies the workings of life systems on the earth creates a powerful logic that, if applied, will pull the economy back from attempting to grow endlessly on a finite planet. The guiding ethic of right relationship that grows out of science establishes a new framework for understanding how the economy itself works.

A New Scientific Understanding Emerges

The new outlook has its roots in the scientific discoveries of the last five hundred years, particularly as they evolved in the nineteenth and twentieth centuries. Taken together, the advances in knowledge in cosmology, physics, and biology form the basis of an emerging understanding or story of humanity's place in the cosmos and in the commonwealth of life.

The emerging cosmological and earth-process story may be said to begin in 1512, when Copernicus demonstrated that it was more plausible that the earth revolved around the sun than the other way around. In the seventeenth and eighteenth centuries, Newton, Kepler, and others demonstrated that the heavens work according to scientific laws that can be discovered by observation, experiment, and inference. They saw the fundamental workings of the universe in terms of locomotion—movement from one place to another—as exemplified in the orderly ellipses of the planets circling the sun.

In the nineteenth century, the discovery of the laws of thermodynamics, which describe changes in state, not just in place, significantly modified this view of a world based on motion. According to the first law of thermodynamics, energy and matter in a closed system can be neither created nor destroyed. This is the idea of the earth as a spaceship. According to the second law of thermodynamics, the entropy law, energy in a closed system is continually and irreversibly transformed from usable to nonreusable forms. This second law explains why highly ordered matter or energy has a natural tendency to become less ordered, as, for example, when a cube of sugar left sitting in a glass of water dissolves. Another aspect of the law states that it will take more energy to put a cube of sugar back together after it dissolves than the energy that was dissipated while the sugar was dissolving. The earth is one of many systems in the universe closed to matter and open to energy from the sun. We now know that the energy that flows from the sun to the earth makes possible virtually all life in all its forms and activities, but in so doing it is gradually and irreversibly dissipated beyond further use.

The next significant marker that now helps science define the new earth-process story was Charles Darwin's *Origin of Species*. Darwin was the discoverer and Thomas Henry Huxley the defender of the theory of the origin of species through natural selection, which, in combination with the work of Gregor Mendel and others, ultimately became what we now call the theory of evolution. After Darwin, humanity's origins were identified as being part of a vast and extremely long process of descent from earlier life forms, with modifications through environmental and sexual selection. Organisms that are better at attracting fertile mates and producing offspring with good survival skills are more likely to pass on their genetic traits. None of the additions and refinements to the theory of evolution and its scientific progeny has undercut the overall evolutionary model; they are merely elaborations of it. Indeed, the theory of evolution has been expanded to include the idea that life on the earth is an agent of change of the planet itself. As life evolves to different forms, it creates and modulates the presence of water, the composition of the atmosphere, the characteristics of the oceans, and the very rock of ages on which everything stands.

For a long time it was puzzling to see how evolutionary discoveries about the increasing complexity of life could be compatible with the second law of thermodynamics. Although entropy drives a natural tendency to dissipate energy and increase disorder, living organisms and ecosystems run in the opposite direction. They harness the steady flow of energy from the sun and make complex, life-sustaining structures that can create still more complexity.

Biodiversity—that is, the sum total of all life forms—because it is capable of discovering multiple pathways to order and complexity, creates life's abundance. As complexity builds, the web of life also creates numerous interlinked pathways for energy to be dissipated. In the formation of the earth and in the development of its commonwealth of life, a continual process of emergence builds up "islands of complexity" in a "sea of entropy." At the level of the organism, the islands of complexity go from microscopic bacteria to giant sequoias and blue whales. At the level of systems and social orders, complexity goes from vast bacterial mats or ant colonies to human economies to the entire interdependent commonwealth of life. Evolution, over the long run, leads to myriad life forms and complex structures, in seeming defiance of the second law of thermodynamics. The answer to why this happens lies in the ability of plants and all other life to harness and simultaneously continuously dissipate the continual stream of sunlight. The sun provides the energy for living things to drive upstream when entropy is pulling in the opposite direction.[1]

The cosmos, therefore, clearly contains a generative process as well as a dissipative process. By influencing these contrasting trends toward complexity and disorder through economic activity and choices, we humans can exercise power to either advance or degrade the integrity, resilience, and beauty of the commonwealth of life. When human numbers on the earth were small, their economic activity, even if locally damaging, had little effect on the integrity of the planet's life-support systems. Plant and animal life was vast and resilient, and human use of it often had a relatively benign effect on the global ecosystem's overall functioning. But today, with nearly 7 billion people and high-energy technology pushing the economy to vastly expanded dimensions, the earth is in a period when the complex systems that life builds are being dismantled faster than they are being put together.

We are in a time of mass, human-caused extinctions that are occurring at a rate a thousand times faster than the normal background rate of species loss.[2] That means that a single life form out of millions—we human beings—are reducing and undercutting the diversity and structure of enormous numbers of entire living ecosystems that support biodiversity, retard erosion, filter pollution, and create more life, among many other things. As fossil fuels are consumed, our activities are decreasing the stock of stored sunlight and changing the climate and other background conditions that affect life's prospects. Moreover, we are appropriating a growing share of the energy flow in general, as the world's forests are depleted and as agriculture and aquaculture expand. All this activity not only leaves less for other species; it also destroys the ground on which they could, otherwise, rebuild their numbers. This ecological crisis is, in effect, an ecological holocaust.

But this is not the only way the human economy can relate to the planet. Our choices regarding economic governance, technology, ethics, and population size can promote *either* ecological degradation *or* ecological preservation and enhancement. The fundamental scientific discoveries that explain why the current economy is on a path toward ecological catastrophe also provide human society with the tools for building a whole earth economy. A significant roster of visionary scientists, economists, and religious thinkers are finding that the emerging cosmological and earth-process story provides a framework for building an economy that enhances life's prospects.

For example, the collaboration of Brian Swimme (a mathematical cosmologist) and Thomas Berry (a theologian and historian of culture) has produced one of the best and most accessible narratives of this new vision, titled *The Universe Story: From the Primordial Flaring Forth to the Ecozoic Era*.[3] Berry followed with the publication of *The Great Work: Our Way into the Future*,[4] which spells out in detail how this "new story" provides a coherent context for the ecologically sound redevelopment of all our life-support and cultural systems.

Stuart Kauffman, a theoretical biologist, and his colleagues at the Santa Fe Institute are revealing the processes of emergence and patterns of relationship that run through energy analysis, information flow, earth science, biological processes, and economic and cultural systems.[5] Biologists Lynn Margulis[6] and evolutionary cosmologist Eric Chaisson[7] have added brilliantly to the "new story" with their explanation of the deep context behind the way the natural and cultural systems of the world actually work.

Integrity and Resilience: Keys to Cosmic Evolution of Ecosystems

In 1869, the German biologist Ernst Haeckel coined the word "œcology," from the Greek *œcos*, meaning house, or household. Haeckel was referring to the notion of the household as a place where numerous organisms live and interact. Ecology eventually emerged as a new science of studying nature's household. The American ecologist Eugene P. Odum was primarily responsible for articulating, in the 1950s, that the ecosystem, or ecological system, is the primary unit of ecological analysis. The study of ecosystems is, therefore, the key to figuring out how to enhance biological diversity through proper care of land and water systems.

Before Odum, in the 1940s Aldo Leopold emphasized ecosystems' integrity and stability. Scientists holding the reductionist view that ecosystems have no properties beyond those of the organisms that make them up initially criticized his focus on integrity. Now, however, scientists understand that the relationships among components of an ecosystem are essential in characterizing it. Others once objected that stability and finality are, in fact, not found in nature. All natural systems, they insisted, are characterized by change, not stability. This debate was resolved through the work of C. S. Holling and others in the closing decades of the twentieth century via the idea of ecological resilience. Ecosystems have functional ranges, defined by characteristics such as temperature, energy flow, species types, and populations. A system is considered to be resilient when it can rebound to its previous functional state after perturbation or disturbance. A nonresilient system is one that cannot rebound to the same or an analogous state. If it cannot rebound, it will likely find a new equilibrium at a lower state of complexity, as could happen to the hayfield at the beginning of this chapter.

The concept of resilience and its many well-examined examples in the real world also demonstrates that ecosystems have self-organizational properties of their own—and are not, therefore, reducible to their component parts. This reformulates Leopold's idea of integrity: A system is healthy when its integrity is resilient. Clearly, if the economy is working in right relationship, a resilient commonwealth of life should be the primary outcome of human economic activity, as well as the primary guide to the moral reformation of economics.

An Emerging Integration of Science, Religion, and Ethics

To understand the extent and character of the current global wasting of the life-building systems on this planet, humanity must rediscover its place in the unfolding drama of the cosmos. More and more scientists, physicists, theologians, and practitioners of traditional belief systems are talking to each other with respect and openness, attempting to create a new, transcending, uniting, and empirically based synthesis of the experience of humans on the earth. Seeing the world in a new way offers a solid basis for a new, unifying guidance system.

For example, physicist Fritz Capra has long turned his expertise to the work of scientific and cultural integration.[8] Indigenous teachers John Mohawk, Oren Lyons, and Jeannette Armstrong, among many others, have helped bring the wisdom and traditions of their peoples about how to live on the earth into broader cultural prominence.[9] Mary Evelyn Tucker and John Grim of the Forum on Religion and Ecology[10] have produced a ten-volume series that gathers historical and contemporary documentation on religious understanding of earth processes and the human–earth relationship. Michel Serres, a French philosopher of science, argues eloquently and passionately for seeing the earth holistically and calls for all peoples to join in a global action "contract" of balance and reciprocity with our common source of life.[11]

Some Implications for Religion

Western civilization, even in its transplanted forms in Africa or the Far East, is in transition from an understanding of the world based primarily on biblical tradition or the traditions of one of the other organized religions in the world, to one informed increasingly by scientific learning about cosmic evolution and earth processes. Cultural transitions often entail serious cultural upheavals. The theologian Thomas Berry says that humanity is in trouble just now because the "Old Story" has become increasingly unbelievable and dysfunctional.[12] A "New Story" is emerging, but it has not yet become a widely recognized guidance system. Western civilization is consequently floundering in confusion about science, ethics, and religion. Collectively, we are lost. As a consequence, all the major religions are experiencing a resurgence in fundamentalist doctrines, belief, and behavior.

A new story offers all people, of any or no faith, the opportunity for a new kind of grounding that does not require them to turn away from the spiritual wellspring of their traditions. Once people begin to assimilate the new scientific understanding of the emergent cosmos and reconcile the human–earth relationship with their deepest beliefs, they will feel a sense of being connected to the deep unity with emergent, creative processes. This is a truly soulful experience, best described by the word "communion." Communion with the purpose of all life is an experience that helps people enlarge their underlying beliefs and refine whatever ethical code currently guides them. In this experience, and in this work, people can gain a sense of co-creation—of playing out, along with the whole community of life, a significant engagement in the unfolding of the earth's story as part of the unfolding universe.

Perhaps the most surprising aspect of the transition from the "Old Story" to the "New Story" is the way the new one transcends the ancient conflict between science and religion. Science is creating a narrative of relationship with regard to the earth and its living environment that is touching the human spirit and enlarging the human sense of morality and ethics. Religion in the West, though previously dominated by a human-centered cosmology and a map of divine intention, is becoming more open to new understandings and to inclusion of scientific discoveries that make literal interpretations of the "Old Story" unbelievable.

Pierre Teilhard de Chardin, a Catholic priest and paleontologist, is a key figure in this rapprochement of religion and science. With the publication of *The Phenomenon of Man* (1955), he set the stage for the next generation of religious thinkers and scientists to see the work of science as "revelatory" of a "new story" that encompasses cosmic, earth, and human narratives. No longer looking to theology for one kind of guidance and to science for another, scholars and researchers such as Thomas Berry, Brian Swimme, John Haught, George Ellis, Nancy Murphy, Ursula Goodenough, E. O. Wilson, and others are taking a new approach. This new approach, looking deeply into the cosmos, finds the human story, and, looking deeply into the human, finds the cosmic story. The earth's history and process is the ground of emergence, complexity, and self-organization in which this narrative of relationship is revealed—which is to say, in plain language, the earth is the source and home of life's great diversity and profound unity.

Swimme and Berry have contributed the concept of "cosmogenesis" to describe how life's complexity unfolds and develops within the earth process. John Haught, a Catholic

> *Earth is the source and home of life's great diversity and profound unity.*

theologian and historian of religion and science (*God After Darwin, Deeper Than Darwin*, and *Is Nature Enough?*), has embraced the story of evolution as adding to the richness of religious narrative. George Ellis, a South African Quaker, mathematician, and prize-winning physicist (*On the Moral Nature of the Universe*, coauthored with Nancy Murphy), has become an international presence in the religion and science dialogue. The biologist Ursula Goodenough (*The Sacred Depths of Nature*) brings the aesthetic response to the world of natural forms and processes fully into alignment with scientific research and analysis. The sociobiologist E. O. Wilson (*Consilience, On the Unity of Knowledge, Biophilia*, and *Creation: An Appeal to Save Life on Earth*), while working as a scientific humanist, has spread such respect, care, and reverence for life throughout his work that he has come to be regarded as a kind of spiritual guide for the human–earth relationship.

The Dalai Lama (*The Universe in a Single Atom*) has been an active participant in the science and religion dialogue, with his particular interest in neuroscience and brain plasticity. He founded the Mind and Life Institute to help advance meditation's contribution to neuroscience research. Starting in 2000 as the Philadelphia Center for Science and Religion, the Metanexus Institute has now become a worldwide network of scholars and scientists, with local chapters in forty-two countries. Metanexus participants generally share the conviction that not only dialogue, but also the active convergence of science and religion, is a much-needed path of world cultural development for human survival. These books and projects are but a sampling of the thought and work that characterizes the growing reconciliation of science and religion as well as the contribution that this cultural change is making to a new, holistic worldview.

Religions typically give prime importance to a reality greater than the individual self, a reality to which awe and respect, and sometimes even love or fear, is due. Guidance is sought and expected from this greater reality, which may or may not be conceived of as God, and which may encompass all of life, and even all that exists. This context and this range of relationships do not disappear with the emergence of the ecological perspective. Each person may reconfigure these experiences and relationships in different ways, but the common element that this new perspective brings into focus is the place of humanity in the cosmos and the way that we human beings all emerge from and are anchored to the great and good gift of the earth. Whatever traditions may inform individual practice, a basic framework of understanding can gather all people in the same "communion":

- We are all part of the same cosmos.
- We live within the commonwealth of life, to which is due the same respect and reverence that we value for ourselves.
- Life's task is to grow in compassion and in a way of living that is helpful to all life, and to the earth systems on which life depends.
- The consequences of failing to live in this sacred manner will diminish our own life value and the well-being of the whole earth community.

Some Implications for Ethics

Most ethical systems evolved and matured before the scientific revolutions of the last several centuries. New scientific understandings challenge or overturn many of those systems' assumptions, especially about the nature of humanity and its place in the universe. As a result, most ethical codes provide "maps of the world" that are no longer very useful for figuring out where one really is. Building a whole earth economy requires rethinking the human place in the world by analyzing some of the key issues in ethics through the perspective of evolutionary biology, thermodynamics, and cosmology. Distributive justice and human rights are examples of ethical issues that make more sense when they account for the findings of science. If science and ethics can be brought together in a mutually enhancing way to provide convincing guidance for ecologically sound behavior, the human story may yet take a positive and more hopeful turn.

The work of two men in the first half of the twentieth century, Albert Schweitzer and Aldo Leopold, pioneered one way to deal with the ethical crisis that current belief systems have created on this planet, at least for Westerners. They endeavored, separately, to create an approach to ethics consistent with modern science, evolutionary biology in particular.[13] They both moved ethics beyond the standard morality that is concerned only with humans. When brought together, their work provides an important synthesis that addresses one of the major weaknesses of modern ethical systems. Schweitzer emphasized duties to living beings that are not human, while Leopold emphasized human duties to biotic communities as whole systems.

Albert Schweitzer was an Alsatian physician and scholar whose life bridged the frontiers of science and religion. He observed that Western ethics got off on the wrong foot a long time ago because it focused on too narrow a question—what is the *human* good? The misstep in Western philosophy that ended up relegating the rest of the natural world to an afterthought was the basic idea that the key problem to be solved was the meaning of life in terms of our species alone. For Schweitzer, a rapprochement between ethics and the theory of evolution seemed essential. He found the key to this connection in the notion of "reverence for life," the need to accord the same deep respect for the will to live in all other living beings that one recognizes in oneself.[14] For him, the commandment to love your neighbor extended to cherishing and helping to both preserve and enhance life's panorama in which you find yourself. With the experience of reverence for life, Schweitzer was thus able to reconcile his Christian ethics with evolutionary biology; Darwin's picture hung above his desk.

Aldo Leopold undertook an intellectual and spiritual journey similar to Schweitzer's. For many years an employee of the U.S. Forest Service, he founded the field of wildlife management. His farm in Wisconsin inspired what is one of the most influential works in conservation of the past century, *A Sand County Almanac*. Although the book is full of biblical references and allusions, Leopold does not depend on any explicit theological doctrine. He is especially critical of the directive to "subjugate" nature that has been traditionally read into the text of Genesis 1:28. To him, the human future depends on seeing land as a community to which people belong, not vice versa. The land itself is a being, in a sense, and we humans have a duty to love and respect it, and especially not to treat it as a commodity.[15] For Leopold, the fundamental principle of ethics can be summarized as set out in this book's introduction: "A thing is right when it tends to preserve the integrity, stability, and beauty of the biotic community. It is wrong when it tends otherwise."[16]

Schweitzer and Leopold were rare Western voices attempting to instill a more holistic ethic of life into a human-centered cultural world. Schweitzer's focus of ethics on the living individual of whatever species, and Leopold's on the systems that make these individual beings possible, will not always yield the same results when applied to particular cases. Should the excess deer that are destroying the young oaks and maples in the forest be culled, or should they be left alone to find their own balance? These kinds of questions remain open in the space outlined by Leopold and Schweitzer. Both were acutely aware that living requires killing. Recognizing this, they turned their attention to how to live with respect and deference to the world around them. The fusion of Leopold's and Schweitzer's ethics helps provide a point of departure, an essential frame of reference for those searching for an enduring moral framework for the economy.

Both these writers and thinkers realized that what is needed in the world they lived in, the Western world, is a deep, widely shared experience of life's unity and great beauty and of humanity's critical role in cherishing, protecting, and enhancing the integrity, resilience, and beauty of all life and life communities. They both took a further step that makes them not simply interesting thinkers, but also spiritual guides to a higher ethical horizon. Their response to life's intensity and to the great beauty of the living world crossed over into love and an impulse to deeply cherish, protect, and nourish individual lives, and also the great tapestry of interdependent life that encompasses the earth. This sense of love and connection is a motivational key. People will protect what they cherish and will nourish what they love. The question of developing a moral economy rests, in part, on whether a sufficient range of key persons find this deep spiritual communion and come together to establish a new ecologically and morally coherent "bottom line" for resource use and for the governance of the common good.

In fact, Schweitzer and Leopold are pioneers of rediscovery. They bring to the fore relationships and ethical guidance that have always been present among many traditional cultures, a number of which still exist in indigenous communities around the world. Their spiritual guidance also lives on in the subsequent work of holistic thinkers like Rachel Carson, whose book *Silent Spring* helped launch the modern environmental movement.

Citizenship in the Commonwealth of Life

A first step in building a whole earth economy involves identifying oneself, both individually and in community, as a citizen in the commonwealth life; Schweitzer and Leopold themselves did this. Humans, one tiny creature living in one tiny neighborhood of one of over a hundred billion galaxies, dwarfed in longevity by bristlecone pines and flummoxed by the engineering ingenuity of social insects, have for many centuries assumed the prerogative to sort out all aspects of the ecosphere in terms of what they think is worth caring for and what they thoughtlessly discard. Citizenship in the commonwealth of life will involve taking a fresh look at what has moral standing and at the duties that we humans have as commonwealth citizens. At its essence, this citizenship calls on each of us to consider the nature of the sacred and to ponder those things to which we owe reverence—is it human life only, or also other forms of life, even all other aspects of creation?

Everyone has duties not only to the individual people or animals that make up ecosystems but to ecosystems themselves. Interdependence is a key feature of the commonwealth of life. Reverence toward natural systems that support human and other life must take into account some knowledge of systems ecology. Modern knowledge of how ecosystems work gives rise to duties to the processes of which humans are a part. Citizenship in the commonwealth of life, then, includes the duty to be stewards of the entire planet—all its systems, all its life forms. If this feels good, all the better; the fact is, it is essential to human survival.

What happens when duties to ecosystems are not respected? The Sumerians founded one of the world's first agricultural civilizations and left behind an almost completely degraded landscape. Ancient Greece denuded its own landscape of forests, then let animals overgraze the land, then overplanted its cash crop, olives, thus permanently impoverishing the soil and its ability to support the cities' former web of life and civilization. It's not hard to imagine a similar end to the story of the tar sands development that opened this book. It is high time to confront the entire range of ecologically unsound adaptations around which human societies are organized. For example, modern industrial agriculture, which devotes large sections of the earth's land surface to poison-soaked monocultures and which actively repels nature's biodiversity, is one of the first systems that needs to be rethought, rescaled, and restructured. Doing so will undoubtedly, in the long run, also entail scaling the human population more wisely within the ecosystems on which each group depends.

An enlightened view of personhood establishes the context for what it means to be a human citizen of the cosmos. We humans are not only products of the universe but agents of its complexity. Is our role in the earth's life processes to be used in support of simplifying or adding complexity to that universe? If humanity as a whole is to succeed as a species, it must advance up the ethical ladder and develop values that reflect reality. These values are emergent systems, resting on other emergent properties, and, like them, the net result of almost 14 billion years of evolution. Indeed, the next ethical stage for humanity is to envision ourselves as custodians of the unfolding of the cosmos that is life on the earth.

An Ecological Update to Keynes's Solution to Economic and Social Instability and Violence

The great English economist John Maynard Keynes devoted his professional life to studying how the economy works. He saw social stability as critically important for the human future. His life spanned the economic crises and catastrophic wars that dominated the first half of the twentieth century, upheavals that carried with them fears that the great advances of Western civilization would be completely lost. In responding to these crises, Keynes saw, correctly, that economic concepts and processes, and often the misunderstanding of their consequences, were a root source of social and economic unrest. In his prescient book *The Economic Consequences of the Peace*, he warned that the Versailles Treaty that brought an end to World War I would push Germany into economic chaos and large-scale unemployment, and would probably lead to the rise of a dictator and another war. As he saw his prediction coming true, Keynes set his hand to the writing of *A General Theory of Employment, Interest and Money*. This work provided the economic foundation for the sixty-year interlude of peace and prosperity that, for the most part, has characterized Europe and some other regions since World War II.

Keynes's central insight was that classical economic theory of the time offered few tools for dealing with systematic unemployment—and thus was largely impotent with regard to heading off political and economic instability. The orthodox theory he challenged contained three postulates: (1) that the supply of goods would create its own demand for labor—by employing the workers that make them, (2) that all money was either spent or invested, and (3) that all unemployment was voluntary. Keynes rejected all three of these ideas. Industrial investment and activity, he said, could in fact stimulate employment, but at levels far below amounts that would employ the bulk of those seeking wages. He also noted that many holders of capital keep their money on the sidelines—in cash, thus providing insufficient investment. Lastly, he rejected the idea that all those who seek a job would find it even if their wage demands were dramatically cut. Under certain circumstances, economies so conceptualized could have high levels of employment, but that was not assured. He demonstrated that the economy could be in an underemployment equilibrium. Indeed, due to the cyclical nature of business activity, social instability would continue to be inevitable.

Keynes argued that classical economic theory, as characterized above, should be seen as a special case. He wished to replace this uneven, unfair, hit-or-miss pattern of economic and social benefits with a general theory of how the economy *could* work. A critical issue during economic downturns was to keep capital robustly deployed. To deal with the problems created by people hiding money in their mattresses (withholding it from circulation), Keynes formulated the idea of the liquidity trap: If investors were concerned that there was about to be a downturn, they, of course, would keep their money out of circulation. So the government had to find ways to assure the holders of capital that their investments would be both safe and rewarded.

For this purpose, Keynes turned to concepts of fiscal and monetary system management. Through managing the money supply and interest rates, investing in or reducing public works and increasing or limiting taxing and spending, government could help dampen the business cycle's extremes. As is now generally seen as normal, in boom times the government would step in to restrain activity (thus avoiding inflationary spirals) by, for example, raising interest rates. In times of economic weakness, government would turn to its instruments of stimulation: lower interest rates, enhanced public works, and so on.

Today's economists continue to debate which of these tools are the best, though they have by and large broken, in critical and unfortunate ways, with Keynes's view of the economy as a means to social stability. His moral vision of what the economy is for—social stability and a good society—and of how it could work toward this end, has been warped into an engine of unlimited growth. His management tools for effecting countercyclical growth of the economy have come to be used as weapons to achieve continuous economic growth for its own sake. The principal dispute today among macroeconomic theorists is over the best way to achieve this constant growth—growth that is undercutting the integrity, stability, resilience, beauty, and even survival of the earth's biotic communities.

Efficiency in a Whole Earth Economy

Keynes's argument from the interwar period needs to be taken in a different direction. Keynes recognized the disruptive effects of large-scale unemployment in Europe and its tendency to spark wars. His corrective for the economy was aimed at stabilizing employment and forestalling violent disruption and social system collapse. The new aim should be broader, grounded in a concern for the current crisis facing the commonwealth of life. A whole earth economy, in addition to fostering social stability, also preserves and enhances the global ecosystem from which the commonwealth of life rises and which, in turn, it sustains. From this point of view, the stimulation of what Keynes called aggregate demand (overall demand)—the principal Keynesian tool for creating employment and thus achieving social stability—must be reevaluated from the perspective of its impact on life's commonwealth.

Efficiency, according to this reevalution, means not only maximizing the satisfaction of human desires subject to constraints (the classic definition given in microeconomics), but also maximizing the products of life's complexity gained, per unit of complexity lost. Or alternatively, efficiency can be used to mean a minimization of complexity lost for a given amount of complexity gained. But it is not just complexity alone that matters—a lake full of algae may be complex, in a sense, but it does not exhibit integrity, resilience, and beauty.

The overall standard of efficiency in a whole earth economy would be derived from the way in which the entire global community of life functions. Reverence for life and respect for every form of life requires that any differential treatment be gauged according to its effect on the integrity, resilience, and beauty of both the overall life-support system and those specific life-support systems that may be involved in economic decision making. Earth efficiency would be the goal of this new economy. Earth efficiency means that economic decision making should compromise life-support systems as little as possible.

Earth efficiency means that economic decision making should minimally compromise life-support systems.

In *Beyond Growth*, Herman Daly describes four kinds of efficiency that are refinements on the umbrella notion of "earth efficiency." Service efficiency concerns the technical design of products and the way they perform. Maintenance efficiency is a measure of durability. Growth efficiency is the ability of ecosystems to replenish themselves. Ecosystem-service efficiency is the measure of how much the functions of ecosystems are disrupted when components are taken from them, or when pollutants are discharged into them. Each of these efficiencies defines a policy space in which people, local communities, nations, and the international community can adopt policies and formulate actions that modify and reduce human impact on life's commonwealth. The overall goal is to reframe the way the economy works in order to satisfy the greatest amount of reasonable human needs and desires with the lowest possible cost to life.

A Whole Earth Economy

An economics for right relationship with the commonwealth of life—a whole earth economy—is built on a narrative that links science with religion and ethics. So far, we have seen that this narrative provides fresh answers to the question, "how does the economy work?" But two subsidiary questions remain: how should we think about wealth and capital, and how should we think about "waste"?

How a Whole Earth Economy Understands Wealth

In a whole earth economy, some common economic terms take on new meaning that reflects how the economy relates to the biosphere. In turn, the concept of wealth, which we now tend to think of in terms of money and what it can buy, also takes on a fundamental new sense. Wealth in a whole earth economy is not monetary wealth, but rather a share of the earth's life and what supports it and keeps it going.

Budgets   Normally, a budget refers to a flow of money—it is a record and often a projection of income and expenses. In a whole earth economy, the primary income is actually sunlight. Spending that sunlight wealth is a matter of using up life and other matter and energy. It's important to remember that the earth's capacity to support life, in part made possible by life itself, is limited but not fixed. Photosynthesis is the primary agent of transformation in support of life, and the primary limiting factors on it are, first, the ability to capture sunlight that is used to create the food, for example, that we humans consume, and to absorb or process the wastes that we throw back into the environment; and second, toxins, which, if allowed to build up in the ecosystem, will affect plants' ability to survive and perform the photosynthesis that keeps us alive. Over the course of life's earthly evolution, some 3.8 billion years, the budget of complexity-creating capacity has, for the most part, been in surplus. That means that life forms have been able to create more apples, more wildebeests, or more sardines than they need to survive, thus feeding other life forms. Substantial deficits occur from time to time, however, such as those associated with the mass extinctions we are now causing.

Comparative Advantage   In a whole earth economy, comparative advantage means a country's or region's ability to transform and consume material and energy with the lowest draw on the earth's life-support capacity. That would suggest that a country that produces goods to sell on the global market at the lowest cost to life's budgets—not the lowest cost in terms of money alone—would become the one with the highest comparative advantage.

Cost   In a whole earth economy, the cost of something is how much of the integrity, resilience, and beauty of the earth's life-support systems must be exchanged to get it. The idea of costs and prices reflects the full cost to life, as measured by the use of net primary productivity (NPP), or other such measures of the earth's life-support capacities.

(Re)Distribution   Claims on shares of the earth's budgets in a whole earth economy are not limited to persons, but can be made by and on behalf of life generally. Distributive justice in terms of distributing wealth—that is, the capacity to build life—therefore applies to the entire commonwealth of life.

Money   In a whole earth economy, money, and its many surrogates like credit, is a socially sanctioned right to intervene, now or in the future, in the earth's life-support budget—in essence, a license to exert an ecological cost by using up complexity or producing wastes and toxins. Inequalities in income and wealth give people various amounts of power over the earth's complexity.

Production/Transformation   The terms "production" and "transformation" normally describe processes of manufacturing or growing something that is useful. In a whole earth economy, there is no actual production of matter, only its transformation. All transformations are net entropic—which means that they increase disorder, or loss of complexity. The concept of "goods" is a partial illusion. All consumption causes a net increase in high-entropy matter or energy—which is what is termed waste.

Resources   What we know as natural resources all play a role in natural systems that human use alters. For example, logging a tree removes habitat and changes ecosystem function; mining metals or tar sands uses up energy and contaminates the environment with substances from beneath the earth's crust. Humanity is a product of evolution and cosmological processes but not their goal, and hence has no special privilege. The earth and the life on it should be looked at as the commonwealth of life—as the result of biological and cosmic evolution, not something made for humanity to use as we see fit.

How a Whole Earth Economy Deals with Waste

From the point of view of a whole earth economy, industrial processes should be analyzed in terms of their effects on the whole commonwealth of life. Industrial processes and waste must be reconceptualized, because there is no production as normally understood—only transformation. The key to applying this principle is to think of costs in terms of elimination of self-organizational capacity or the interference with recovery—as with toxins that impede life's resilience, toxins released, say, in a manufacturing process. Every time something is made, a waste stream is created, and the energy used in that making process always declines in its ability to do work. Waste is the inability to do any more work to maintain self-organizational capacity.

Once the world's interconnected ecological limits are accounted for, the internalization of materials, not their cost (as it is traditionally understood), becomes paramount.[17] Karl-Henrik Robèrt and his colleagues in the Natural Step Movement in Sweden have formulated the basic principles involved in this approach to manufacturing and materials handling, and they are being used in scores of industries and countries around the world, the manufacturing giant Ikea being one of the main practitioners:[18]

- Materials from within the earth's crust, the lithosphere, should not be allowed to accumulate systematically in the surface environment. Heavy metals like lead and cadmium are good examples of materials that must be sequestered to protect life.

- Materials from human society should not accumulate in the biosphere. Tens of thousands of human-made compounds are now accumulating in the biosphere. This is, in part, attributable to current economic systems and behavior. Since markets for many existing products are satiated, stimulating further consumption requires novelty to inspire consumers to buy the new item. Product innovation depends, in many sectors, on chemical engineering that introduces novel and insufficiently tested substances into the environment. Those who want to introduce new substances should have the burden of showing that their impact on life's commonwealth would be benign; if they can't, they should not be allowed to produce them.

- Society must not systematically deplete or degrade natural systems. For example, the ocean's fish stocks should be kept abundant, forest cover kept intact, water and air kept unpolluted, and soil fertility maintained.

- As discussed in Chapter 4, people should not be subjected to conditions that systematically undermine their ability to meet their needs. This means, among other things, sufficient income, decent housing, meaningful work or other ways to contribute to society, access to education, adequate health care, and social opportunities for satisfying and nurturing relationships.

A wide variety of manufacturing companies and communities around the world have adopted the Natural Step program for several decades now without suffering any serious economic disadvantage.[19] This is a prime example of the already growing whole earth economy.

Sewage provides a good example of how a new concept of waste would work in a whole earth economy. In most industrialized countries, sewage is regarded as something to be gotten rid of. Indeed, one of the most substantial advances in human health was brought about by keeping sewage segregated from water supplies, so there can be no quarreling with this outcome. Yet, if kept separate from chemical toxins, which is unfortunately not the case with sewage systems in North America (as only one example), pure sewage would not be real "waste" but an asset out of place. Sewage contains the results of photosynthesis. In its natural state, it is a resource that for centuries has been and still can be reinvested in the earth's limited capacity for the production and sustenance of life.

The Path to a Whole Earth Economy

The open horizon of what Kenneth Boulding called the "cowboy economy" of the 1980s (that of the laissez-faire capitalists, the market fundamentalists) has changed to the limited horizon of the "spaceman economy."[20] We are fortunate indeed that we have a narrative with which to reenvision the future, and a little time, as well as some of the conceptual tools needed to begin a fundamental rethinking. Yet this is just the very beginning. Questions of scale, equity, and governance are dealt with next.

How Big Is Too Big? Boundaries on Consumption and Waste

How serious is the threat to the environment? Here is one measure of the prob-
lem: all we have to do to destroy the planet's climate and biota and leave a
ruined world to our children and grandchildren is to keep doing exactly what we
are doing today, with no growth in the human population or the world economy.
Just continue to release greenhouse gases at current rates, just continue to im-
poverish ecosystems and release toxic chemicals at current rates, and the world
in the latter part of this century won't be fit to live in. But, of course, human ac-
tivities are not holding at current levels—they are accelerating, dramatically.

—James Gustave Speth, *The Bridge at the Edge of the World*[1]

THE ECONOMY IS IN right relationship with the commonwealth of life when it respects ecological limits and thresholds. Living within certain bounds is something we can all relate to. Imagine a typical home in Sweden in the thick of winter. Obviously, this home needs an external source of energy to be habitable. Yet, unless the home has a system to control the heat source, it will become either too hot or too cold. A thermostat keeps the temperature of the home within a habitable range. In a similar but much more complex way, the economy needs a set of controls to make sure that the countless interactions that make up the economy, taken together, use the matter and energy available on the earth on a scale that maintains right relationship with the commonwealth of life. Right relationship involves a quest for figuring out the right scale of the economy, and then respecting its key limits and thresholds.

Economic interactions all require some amount of energy and matter. Even a simple act like walking to the corner store to buy a carton of milk depends on a whole series of uses of material and energy. The food you ate to enable you to walk, the clothes you wear, the sidewalk, the building the store is in, the cow that produced the milk, the packing and transporting of the milk to the store, the paper money or coins used to pay for the milk, and so on: All those things take a certain amount of matter and energy. These interactions are also interdependent. For example, your buying milk at the corner store is connected in some way to all the interactions of the farmer who produced the milk and the owner of the store who sold it to you. Did the farmer feed growth hormones or antibiotics to the cow? Did he use fossil fuel–derived pesticides or fertilizers to produce the cow's feed? Did the store owner buy the milk from nearby, or from far away?

These interactions are also connected to what you do with the energy and substance you gain from drinking the milk. Buying milk from the corner store is a relatively simple example. Leasing a car, going to college, or constructing an office building involves more complicated chains of interlinked uses of material and energy. Imagine all the economic interactions, and all the matter and energy, involved in the international arms trade or waging war. Or walk into a Wal-Mart or a Costco: How many interlinked chains of uses of matter and energy do the rows and rows of stuff you see account for?

Now, recall that our planet is closed to matter and open to energy from sunlight. The countless transactions that make up the global economy all draw on sources and sinks of matter and energy, and all those sources and sinks have limits. In the milk example, the grass that feeds the cow is transformed into milk, which when drunk by a person is further transformed, and then much of it, quite probably, is flushed down the toilet. The earth's capacity to provide the grass (and today the grains and chemicals) that feed cows (the source), as well as the capacity to process matter that is flushed down toilets (the resource sink), is finite. Even if matter is used over and over through the cycles of life, those cycles also take time. The countless sources and sinks of energy and matter involved in the economy also interact in countless ways. Sticking with the milk example, suppose the cow pasture is downwind of a chemical plant that emits toxic fumes. The soil in the pasture is not only a source for the grass that feeds the cows, but also a sink for the toxins in the chemical plant emissions. What happens to your milk when too much of those toxins rain down into the soil?

Just as a thermostat keeps a house's temperature within a certain range, the ecological limits of all the sources and sinks involved in the economy, plus their interactions, describe the limits within which life's commonwealth must remain, so that it can survive and flourish in the long run. The key to determining those limits is the rate at which all this matter and energy is processed through the economy. This throughput depends on how many people there are, multiplied by how much energy and matter each person uses, and how fast. Ultimately, the limits on the economy's scale come down to how much of the earth's photosynthetic production and how much of natural systems' capacity to process waste we humans, individually and collectively, may legitimately appropriate or interfere with. Exceeding these limits causes finite resources to be depleted, ecosystems to break down, toxins and other pollutants to build up, and life communities to be destroyed. Climate change offers a good illustration of what happens when scale limits are exceeded—and temperature is only one signal of when the earth's ecology is out of whack.

What are the other signals? If biodiversity goes down—that is, if species are lost—that can be a strong sign of an out-of-scale economy. The amounts of pollutants in the air and water, deforestation, desertification, ecosystem function, and many other indicators of the health of the ecosphere all point to an economy with a thermostat that's turned up too high. Although they are more abstract, the concepts of integrity, resilience, and beauty are also essential to finding a right relationship between the human economy and the earth's limits and thresholds. An economy that is out of bounds—too big, too small, too invasive, too intense, too momentous—will have a negative effect on the integrity, resilience, and beauty of the social systems and ecosystems that make up life's commonwealth.

> *An out-of-bounds economy will have a negative effect on the social systems and ecosystems that make up the commonwealth of life.*

Limits on the Sources and Sinks of Economic Activity

Sunlight is the economy's fundamental driver. Chapter 2 explained how, one way or another, the sun fuels almost all the biological processes that allow living things to form, interact, and maintain complexity, despite the entropic tendency toward disorder. Because we humans so far have developed only a modest ability to capture sunlight directly, we generally use the sun's energy that is stored in fossil fuels or captured by plants. The capacity of the earth and the sun to produce these inputs to the economy is limited: You can only grow so many watermelons, and oil and coal undoubtedly will run out long before the sun and slow-moving geological processes can make more. The sun also controls the ability of the earth's geophysical and biological systems to absorb waste. Here, too, there are limits. Natural systems can absorb or process only so many by-products of human activity before they break down. In other words, the sun *both* feeds our needs and desires *and* cleans up our messes, but with limits. A whole earth economy can preserve and enhance an ecosphere that supports life and its evolution only by staying within these solar-powered limits.

So what are the ecological limits on the scale of the economy?[2] In terms of the sources that feed economic transactions, the key limit is the ability to capture sunlight's energy and use it to support biological complexity. This limit is a moving target: We are getting better and better at using solar panels and other technologies that allow direct use of the sun's energy, which is a good thing. The sun is also the underlying controlling factor for other limits in the complex systems that make up and sustain life. As the fishing community in Newfoundland knows all too well, fish stocks have a limited ability to replenish themselves after too many have been consumed by humans. As the orangutans of Borneo and Sumatra and myriad forms of life in the Amazon are also discovering, to our and their sadness, forests have a limited ability to recover from both natural disturbances such as fires or wind storms and unnatural disturbances such as war, climate change, timber harvesting, or contamination by genetically modified organisms. Dust Bowl farmers in Oklahoma found out in the 1930s that once their grasslands' topsoil was exposed to wind erosion and blown away, the ecosystem's ability to restore soil and its fertility was beyond the timescale of their economy. The debate over whether global oil production has already peaked is a debate about *when*, not whether, oil will run out. The ability of all these systems to generate and regenerate their defining features is finite.

Other limits have to do with the ecosphere's ability to clean up any messes that humans or other species may make. The climate change crisis has to do with limits on the ability of natural systems, like the oceans and tropical forests, to make use of greenhouse gases so as to maintain stable concentrations of them in the atmosphere. People in the Middle East and the American West are rapidly discovering the limits on the number of users (human or others) and uses that freshwater systems can accommodate without deteriorating or running out. The so-called Brown Haze over central Asia and the growing dead zone where the Mississippi River enters the Gulf of Mexico are evidence of the limited ability of air and water to disperse pollutants. The American bald eagle's close brush with extinction and the ongoing controversy over burying nuclear waste in Nevada are reminders of the time it takes nuclear material and complex chemicals, like pesticides, to decay or break down. The disturbing growth of female sex organs in male freshwater fish in many parts of the world is due to ecosystems' limited ability to tolerate toxins, endocrine disrupters, and other pollutants without loss of function or biodiversity. Likewise limited is natural systems' ability to remain healthy after nonindigenous or genetically engineered organisms or the products of nanotechnology are introduced into the environment.

By being set up in the first place to operate well within these physical limits, an economy that is in right relationship would allow both natural and human communities to flourish. Most of the concern today is about the economy's being too big to be in right relationship with life's commonwealth. But the economy can also be too small. It has to be big enough to support basic needs for whatever the human population is, once it becomes appropriately limited based on respect for the basic needs of future generations of humans *and* the current and future generations of other species.

Ideal scale is not just a question of size; speed, momentum, and intensity also matter. How fast change occurs affects the ability of life's communities to adapt. Ecosystem function is more likely to be preserved when, for example, climate change is slow and there is time to adapt. Momentum has to do with the sheer mass of an environmental impact; and some environmental impacts carry vast momentum. The earth, for example, would continue to warm for centuries even if all fossil fuel emissions were to stop today. The size of the human population also has enormous momentum; even with drastically reduced human fertility rates, the population would still continue to climb before starting to fall. The intensity of human activity also matters, because the impact of human intervention generally increases as it is compressed in time or space. The atomic bombs dropped on Hiroshima and Nagasaki are horrific reminders of how intense human impacts can be. The speed, intensity, and momentum with which human-generated changes occur are capable of permanently overwhelming the natural rhythms that are affected, because ecosystem resilience is limited.

Taking a broad look at the current state of sources and sinks in the biosphere that support human economic activity, we can see that the economy today is clearly out of scale. True, human impacts are not always negative. People can and do help life flourish, for example through the controlled use of fire, well-managed harvesting of plant and animals, terrace agriculture, carbon-neutral green buildings that minimize and recycle waste, and many other human activities such as wildlife and biodiversity preserves that have historically added to, rather than subtracted from, the integrity, resilience, and beauty of life's commonwealth.

However, the most cheerful optimist could not be blamed for having mixed views on whether we human beings will come to terms with the current set of ecological threats facing the world in time to avoid serious, unprecedented, widespread human-caused ecological disaster. Phenomena long in the making, such as climate change[3] and mass extinction, are interacting with other looming global trends—in particular, overpopulation—to pose a frightening set of ecological crises that often seem impossible to overcome. The earth is experiencing an unprecedented convergence of a series of trend lines that for millennia have been nearly flat and in only the past century, and particularly since World War II, are suddenly surging upward at dramatic rates: human population, consumption, species extinctions, and especially CO_2 concentration in the atmosphere, which is a leader among these trend lines.[4]

Efforts to look at these trends in the aggregate, for example in the UN Millennium Ecosystem Assessment initiated in 2000,[5] show that humans are using the biosphere's capacity to produce what people and other living things consume and to assimilate pollutants and other remnants of economic activity considerably faster than the biosphere is able to regenerate. Humans, and indeed the entire commonwealth of life, are now running a growing ecological deficit. The longer this goes on, the bigger the ecological debt that will be left for future generations of life's commonwealth. The problem is, this ecological debt cannot be paid off with the kind of hard-cash bailouts that have become the typical response to the collapse of a financial bubble. It will be collected in the form of unthinkable losses of human and other life. Indeed, the bill collector is already at the door.

The record of unintended consequences in the history of human economic development gives additional causes for concern. Technological or other economic solutions often cause new, even more complicated problems. For example, the disturbing legacy of exotic species, introduced intentionally or by accident in new ecosystems, is now very well known. One such species illustrates the problem well. Quick-growing melaleuca trees, imported from Australia and planted as windbreaks on south Florida farms, are now spreading across the Everglades, displacing native plant species and robbing other marsh life of precious water. Who knew that efforts to destroy these trees with fire would, instead, cause their fire-resistant seeds to explode and spread further? Humans try hard to outsmart nature but quite often fall short. What, for example, are the unknowns and miscalculated assumptions involved in the development and release into natural systems of genetically or nanoscopically manipulated organisms?

Scale and Integrity

Integrity has to do with the ecological health of systems. Ecosystems that have integrity are efficient, holistic, and balanced. The living organisms in a healthy ecosystem make the optimum use of the energy and matter in the system to build complexity, which in turn is optimized to seek out the best pathway toward entropy-driven disorder. This is why the air above healthy tropical rainforests is cool. The organisms in the forest are using up the heat of the sun for their own life purposes. An ecosystem with integrity interacts in a healthy way with other ecosystems with which it is interdependent.

Of course, an arctic ecosystem does not behave the same way as a tropical one. The integrity of any particular ecosystem depends on such things as its latitude, its soil, geological features, wind patterns, temperature, precipitation patterns, and so on.

The degraded Everglades in south Florida might be seen as quite resilient, but whether they have retained their integrity is another question. Elaborate civil engineering projects—dikes, canals, the largest pumps in the world—have transformed the former river of grass that once swept south from Lake Okeechobee. The Everglades were once an extremely low-nutrient system with immense expanses of saw grass interspersed with profusions of life around bird rookeries, alligator holes, and other local sources of nutrients. They are now a battleground among an entire series of users who want possession of these resources: agricultural interests that farm what was once the northern reach of the marsh, burgeoning cities along the Atlantic coast, Native American tribes trying to preserve their homes in the marsh, and the native plant and animal species that adapted to conditions that are becoming harder and harder to maintain.

Nutrients flowing south from agricultural lands have converted saw grass stands to cattail, a species that outcompetes saw grass, once low-nutrient conditions disappear. Beds of sea grass off the southern reach of the Everglades are dying off. Exotic species like melaleuca exact a different toll by drying up the marsh; drainoff from cities does more. The network of interlocking devastation is vast. Degraded portions of the Everglades that rebound are likely now along a different path, which means that changing back to the former natural state would be difficult, if not impossible. Those parts of the Everglades may still have some resilience, but they have lost their integrity.

The Everglades is just one small part of the global picture of what is happening to the integrity of ecosystems worldwide. An overview of the ecological hotspots on a global level provides a picture of the overall integrity of the earth's life systems, and offers a devastating idea of what there will be more of unless a new approach is taken as quickly as possible. Many measures of ecosystem health have been developed, and they will be increasingly important tools as we build a whole earth economy that maintains the integrity of the earth's life systems.[6]

Scale and Resilience

Living systems are never static. Instead, they are constantly reacting to disturbances and changing variables, in perpetual evolution from one state to another. The life of a creek is on a new course when a beaver builds a dam, just as it is when an industrial cattle farm is located nearby. At some point, change can be significant enough that the entire functioning of the system changes, and a new system emerges.

Resilience is the ability to maintain a system's integrity and overall function in response to changing conditions. Resilience can be complicated, because a change in conditions is not necessarily cause for concern. When a beaver builds its small dam across a creek, the area affected adapts relatively quickly, and not only does it remain rich with life but new species appear. When humans build a large dam, the effect on the immediate surroundings is also acute and significant, and that is just the beginning of a chain of consequences, but usually one that causes a decrease in life forms. Vast stores of methane are released into the atmosphere as vegetation rots. The cycle of life in the river will likely be adversely affected hundreds of miles downstream by changes in flow and turbidity. The irrigation, electricity, and other end uses the dam allows all have their own series of ecological consequences. The key is to figure out what kinds of impacts from the human economy so undermine biological systems' resilience as to threaten their ability to support and maintain the commonwealth of life.

Figuring out measures of resilience is not merely an academic exercise. At some point, enough systems will be affected that the economy, which is embedded in the commonwealth of life, will be destroyed as well. Recent research has shown how the Maya in Yucatan, the Anasazi in the American Southwest, the Cahokia mound builders in southern Indiana, the Greenland Norse, the statue builders of Easter Island, the ancient Mesopotamians in the Fertile Crescent, and the people of Great Zimbabwe in Africa and of Angkor Wat in Cambodia all passed beyond this breaking point.[7] Today, the test of the resilience of the economy and the systems it depends on is playing out on a global scale.

In thinking about resilience, a major question that has to be answered is how big the overall economy can be before conditions change so fundamentally that the ecological systems the economy depends on function in different, less productive, and less resilient ways. A problem like climate change threatens the biosphere's resilience because of the sheer quantity of greenhouse gas emissions. However, the size of the disruption is not the only factor. Resilience also depends on the intensity and invasiveness of the economic transactions that lead to such changes, as well as on the speed at which they occur. Humans may cause enormous damage to life with a tiny amount of plutonium, exploded with great intensity in a nuclear explosion. Likewise, materials or organisms altered through nanotechnology, or affected at the molecular level by genetic engineering, can severely affect the resilience of life systems, even if they are not produced in mass quantities.

Tracking ecosystem resilience is complex because natural systems typically cycle through four main phases: rapid growth, conservation, release, and reorganization.[8] For example, a forest begins this cycle with a profusion of growth, which then levels off before the forest goes through a period of increased die-off, which in turn enriches the soil so that it can support a new cycle of growth. Because systems behave differently in each phase, it is important to know what phase the system is occupying, in order to predict how it will react to changes. It is also important to understand how one system is linked with others and how those systems are behaving. A tree is part of a forest, which is part of a watershed, which is part of a landmass, which is part of the entire earth. With a good understanding of these characteristics of the system, it is possible to find opportunities to influence systems in beneficial ways, rather than harming them.

The resilience of a system often depends on key variables, that is, drivers of change that can move the system to a complete shift in function. For example, the aquatic system in a lake is highly dependent on the nutrient level in the water. A change from low-phosphorous to high-phosphorous levels in a lake completely alters the kinds and diversity of aquatic life in that lake. After a point, a threshold is crossed, and returning to the prior state is difficult, if not impossible. Many parts of the Everglades, to return to a previous example, have likely crossed this threshold. Scale questions turn on these key variables and their thresholds.[9]

System resilience also depends on diversity. Simplifying a system to promote efficiency yields higher short-term returns in some respects, but usually weakens the overall resilience of the system. Over the past fifty years, foresters around the world have learned that a diverse, old-growth forest can withstand disturbance from disease or fire far better than an even-aged forest with few species. Monocultures in agriculture, such as the single species of livestock that are raised in industrial farms to produce beef, pork, and poultry, become highly vulnerable to disease, and require increasing amounts of antibiotics and containment to maintain. In economic systems, higher resilience can mean lower short-term profits, but better adaptability and resistance to crisis over the long term.

Scale and Beauty

The beauty of the commonwealth of life might seem hopelessly subjective, and therefore almost impossible to define, or to include along with integrity and resilience as an essential component of right relationship. Aldo Leopold, however, proposed a definition of beauty that linked it to the idea of "land health," which he defined as "the capacity for self-renewal in the biota."[10] Leopold's notion of beauty is consistent with the view of biologists, that personal beauty, as perceived by potential mates, is related to genetic and reproductive fitness,

> *The beauty of the commonwealth of life is linked to land health, the capacity for self-renewal in the biota.*

one major attribute of which is personal health. When tied to notions of health and vitality, beauty is measurably objective, not just "in the eye of the beholder." At the same time, beauty has elements of the wonder that comes from acknowledging us humans as being an integral part of the earth's life systems, and of the earth as part of the evolving universe. We can think of beauty in this context, therefore, as the aesthetic appreciation of resilience and integrity.

Of course, different cultures (and certainly individuals) have different concepts of beauty. The overall narrative of a culture informs what it considers to be beautiful. In much of modern Western culture, the underlying narrative has been supplied by an economy based on "bigger," "faster," and "more." The kind of beauty that is loaded into much of advertising is built on this narrative: "You just have to have this shiny SUV to drive up those twisting mountain roads—It's a beauty!" There's even a current ad that asserts that the most Perfect Moment of life is to be found in driving a Lexus at high speed, meaning there is literally nothing one could seek that could be more wonderful or more profound. But beauty built on wrong relationship with the commonwealth of life is a false kind of beauty. Recognizing this, writers such as Lewis Mumford[11] and Jane Jacobs[12] have argued, with limited success within our current culture, for the design of spaces with a human scale—spaces that reinforce human contact and community; that is, spaces conducive to right relationship with others. Jacobs's concept of vibrant urban space is reminiscent of Darwin's phrase "nature's entangled bank,"[13] a resplendent display of the creative powers of life.

People who understand ecosystems in their evolutionary and cosmic context are people who live in a "world of wounds," to use

Leopold's phrase. At nearly every turn they can find thoughtlessness, violence to other beings on the planet, a palpable lack of caring that is painful to the beholder. In many ways, it is the aesthetic reaction to these wounds that has been the impetus for many of the successful conservation efforts that have occurred. People think, "This denuded hillside or filthy river is ugly; this cannot be right." Beauty based on right relationship is a springboard for changing our perception from one of exploiter to one of steward—that is, to one who restores, nourishes, and brings forth the flourishing of life's commonwealth.

Analyzing the Key Variables: A Look at I=f(PATE)

The main variables by which we affect the integrity, resilience, and beauty of the commonwealth of life are population, affluence, technology, and ethics. The framework I=f(PATE), a modification of the formula I=f(PAT) developed by Paul Ehrlich and John Holdren in 1971,[14] offers a way to consider these variables, where human impact (I) is a function (f) of population (P), affluence (A), technology (T), and ethics (E). Think of human impact as a measure of how the economy is affecting the integrity, resilience, and beauty of the commonwealth of life. For a whole earth economy, there is a limit on how big the human impact (I) can be if we are to keep it from overwhelming the commonwealth of life. Changes in practice and policy need to be organized around these four variables—they define the theaters of opportunity to build a whole earth economy.

These variables interact with each other, so it is important not to think of I=f(PATE) as a simple formula where you just multiply together P, A, T, and E to get the human impact on the environment.[15] An economy in right relationship with the earth's life systems must account for the *interrelationships* that exist among these variables, which are complex and do not lend themselves to easy mathematical manipulation. It is also important to determine which variables are most important. For example, if further gains in technological efficiency seem unlikely, then we need to focus more on adjusting the other three variables.

The I=f(PATE) framework sets up a number of ways for thinking about how the economy, examined along scales of quantity, velocity, and intensity, affects the commonwealth of life. How much and what kind of production and consumption of food, energy, and natural resources do ecological limits require and allow? How much and what kind of waste generation? How much wilderness and biodiversity should be maintained? How many humans can inhabit the earth? The answers to fundamental questions like these will establish the scale of an economy in right relationship with the earth's life systems.

Population With respect to human population, the upper limit on the size of the economy can be viewed two ways. Given a fixed human population, the size of the economy is determined by the affluence, technology, and ethics variables. To put this another way, if A, T, and E are fixed, the human population (P) can only be so high until the impact (I) of the economy becomes too big. As population increases, the range of options for maintaining a whole earth economy gets more and more limited. As P increases, the A, T, and E variables must be adjusted if impact (I) is to stay the same; or, as is actually required now, population must substantially decrease. From a current population of almost 7 billion, some estimates project the human population increasing to about 10 to 12 billion before it stabilizes.[16] Human population projections are more concrete than figures attempting to summarize the affluence, technology, and ethics variables, and therefore population is the logical starting point for determining the adjustments in the other variables that will be needed to maintain a resilient planet. In other words, if those other variables cannot carry the burden of keeping the human impact at an acceptable level—and it is not likely that they can—the population must decrease.

Studies of the human ecological footprint, along with the science of climate change, species extinctions, the state of water resources, and other bad news from the science front, strongly indicate that, given the current state of the A, T, and E variables, the human population is already far too large. The earth's ability to support life's complexity is being torn down faster than sunlight and photosynthesis can build it back up. Because affluence tends to correlate with consumption, each new wealthy European or North American, for example, at this point in time is likely to be a curse for the planet rather than a blessing. At the same time, countries with vast and rapidly growing populations, such as India and China, will exact an unfair toll on the biosphere and future generations of humans if they continue rushing toward more affluence without reducing their birthrates sufficiently to reduce their populations.

Affluence   Wealth and poverty both have a relationship with ecological impact. Money is a license that society has created to allow people to enter into transactions that have a social and ecological impact. Everything else being equal, people with more of it will have a greater ecological impact. They will have larger homes, take vacations in remote places requiring vast amounts of fuel to reach, demand stylish foods that must be imported from other ecosystems, run electric dryers rather than hang clothes on lines, and so on. But large numbers of people living in poverty can also cause severe damage to the earth's life-support systems. For example, even though the rich are responsible for the vast majority of deforestation and for the erosion, floods, and habitat loss that deforestation causes, high numbers of poor people gathering wood to cook with or in search of land to farm can also have these impacts. If they had access to solar stoves, for example, or some kind of equitable tenure on the vast acreages that are industrially managed with as few people as possible by big corporate operations, many of these harms could be avoided. Right relationship means that people should be neither too rich nor too poor.

One of the factors that has led to the rise of vast affluence in many countries is the mass production of manufactured goods. This has been made possible by economies of scale. The general principle behind economies of scale is that it is more economically efficient for one producer to produce large quantities of something than for many small units to, collectively, produce the same quantity. Large producers can make their capital yield more products than the same amount of capital spread out among several small producers. But what are the hidden consequences of "economies of scale" for the collective, human ecological footprint? How far do the resulting goods or their inputs have to be shipped from large, centralized centers of production? What by-products of manufacture go up the smokestack and fall down into rivers, lakes, and oceans? Increasing efficiency to increase short-term profits can reduce resiliency in the long term. Within the context of a whole earth economy, the idea of economies of scale has to be embedded within the ecological limits of the earth.

Technology Impact can be reduced in numerous ways via technology. For example, insulating your house is one way to get more warmth for a given amount of firewood, fuel oil, or natural gas. Lining or covering canals to decrease water transport losses to leakage and evaporation can help conserve scarce water resources. Green buildings that use less energy and more environmentally benign materials than conventional buildings in their construction and operation can reduce the ecological footprint of our built environment. Cars that consume little or no fossil fuels help reduce global warming, as do solar and other renewable energy technologies. Long-term development and widespread application of technologies and practices that virtually eliminate waste by using a "waste is food" or "cradle-to-cradle" principle could help reduce the human ecological footprint.

The modern economy has been driven, in part, by the prevailing view that as natural resources are depleted or technology is discovered to have harmful effects, we humans are infinitely creative and will always develop new technologies to get ourselves out of trouble.[17] Yet technological optimism, which is a form of blind faith that technology alone will solve our ecological crisis, can be extremely dangerous. First, consider the problem of side effects. Cars, whether fuel-efficient or not, are still vastly destructive in terms of highways that fragment ecosystem integrity, parking lots that render resilience impossible, and destruction of the beauty and tranquility of the landscape. Second, new technologies often create new burdens. Witness the disasters caused by the promotion of biofuels to run our cars. This "green technology" helped hike food prices and resulted in conversion of ecologically sensitive land to agricultural monocultures. Third, there is a problem of delay and false confidence. The whole concept of leaning back and waiting for experts to develop ways to bury CO_2, raise fish in ponds on land, build cars that run on hydrogen or sun power, and create genetically modified organisms that will adapt to climate change is extremely problematic. Maybe these ideas will work, maybe they won't. Maybe they *will* work, but will come too late. In the meantime their prospect is used to avoid responsible action in the present.

The burden that new forms of technology must carry becomes increasingly heavy as the human population and overall affluence increases. Technological innovations need to be approached in the context of a deep humility that takes into account the very spotty human record when it comes to interventions in natural systems. Many well-intentioned new technologies—CFCs, the widespread use of motor vehicles, and pesticides leap to mind—have proven to be massively, irreversibly damaging to us humans and to our fellow creatures of the biosphere.

Finally, consideration of the *T* factor requires acknowledgment of the Jevons Paradox,[18] which is the principle that improvements in efficiency that result from new technologies often encourage even greater consumption of the energy or material conserved. Thus, electricity saved by installing efficient light bulbs might be squandered on an air conditioner; people might feel better taking longer trips once they have fuel-efficient vehicles. Ironically, in the context of the kind of economy now in operation, increased efficiency can result in even more consumption and hence greater impact.[19] It is painful but true: Technology alone will not save life's commonwealth. Changes in wealth, population, and behavior are much more essential.

Ethics People who can easily afford not to may nonetheless decide to recycle, take the bus, grow some of their own food, or vacation close to home instead of on the other side of the world. Ethical issues, which include moral values associated with different cultures, can have quite substantial effects on human impact on the environment. Obviously, many of the world's traditional cultures have much less impact per person than do the consumption-based cultures of Europe and North America. Much of this is due to poverty. However, lower per-capita consumption can also result from a shift in ethical standards. Given what is known about the human desire to conform with the values of society, if an ethic of right relationship were to become the norm, human impact would, everything else being equal, decline significantly. Industrial animal agriculture as a means of getting meat would be eliminated on the basis of considerations of reverence for life alone; this is already happening in the growing movement to eat locally grown and ethically produced food, beautifully described in Barbara Kingsolver's book *Animal, Vegetable, Miracle.*[20] The commitment of tens of millions of acres of land to grow corn for feedlots and automobile fuel would not pass muster when subjected to the test of right relationship. Driving a gas-guzzling Hummer would be unimaginable. And having on average more than one child per couple, at least until population reaches levels at which an economy in harmony with the global ecosystem is possible, would be unethical.

The ethics factor in the $I=f(PATE)$ framework is tied to how people think of tolerance and freedom. One of the greatest sources of the present time's tragedies is how the idea of tolerance has played out. In his *Letter on Toleration*, one of seventeenth-century English philosopher John Locke's principal arguments is that matters of religious belief are private. Hence the state may take no legitimate interest in them. So far, so good. But in the current consumer culture, the religion that the state must tolerate, but also actively promotes, is the religion of consumption: "I may live my life as I wish, and my

The religion that the state must tolerate and actively promotes is that of consumption.

freedom of expression includes whatever I choose to consume and display, which is therefore exempt from societal control." Society has increasingly tolerated this total freedom of consumption because of a deep-rooted belief in two things: first, Adam Smith's "invisible hand," the market's supposed inherent ability to adjust prices, supply, and demand to the perfect amount and variety of goods and services; and second, people are rational economic actors, with perfect knowledge of all the relevant information about the impacts of economic choices on themselves, other people, and the environment.

But the rational actor that economists rely on to promote the free-market economy exists only in the theories of free-market economists. Behaviorial economics, a specialty that has arisen in recent years, has shown through experiments and empirical studies that people often make decisions that are irrational, or that they start their decision making from a point that is greatly influenced by irrelevant information. People buying lottery tickets, despite the extremely low odds of winning, or the remorse that winning bidders feel at auctions, are examples of emotional and impulse reactions to consumption. Nonetheless, the power of the economist's fictional rational actor is strong—policy makers are highly resistant to promoting options that can be seen to cut off choice in any way. Further, advertising, so pervasive around the globe today, is designed to continuously create escalating desires that the supposedly rational consumers did not even know they had.

The view of freedom in the United States and elsewhere is highly relevant to the ethical variable in the I=f(PATE) framework. The inducement to buy and consume incessantly comes not merely from paid advertisements, but also from television shows around the world, as well as most movies, in which audiences are tantalized by visions of extremely opulent human lifestyles. Advertising promotes a level of consumption that is far out of reach even for the typical American household, not to mention families in the rest of world. The techniques of the advertising culture used in the service of unending consumption grow in sophistication and subtlety by the day. Commercial messages fill every environment except the most rural or remote, encroaching on personal space in restaurants, e-mails, and even restrooms. All the while, marketing companies track habits and spending patterns, which enables them to target individual consumers more effectively, thus reinforcing addictions and creating new desires.

The culture of advertisement and consumption drives public support for a growth agenda, and also for the social idea that any kind of sharing will impede the chances of becoming one of the very rich. The vast majority of political and societal leaders and the media tell their constituents that the only way to obtain all the things the rich have today is for the economy to keep on growing. Of course, that goal is always shifting upward, from "a chicken in every pot" to two cars in every garage, five telephones, and a huge wide-screen, high-def TV. The never-ending extension of desire totally ignores the pressure that mass desires place on finite resources of every kind.

Ideas of freedom and personal well-being must be felt from within. This is a central challenge when we consider the ethical prong of the I = f(PATE) framework. A concept of freedom built on right relationship could lead to an increasingly widespread blossoming of the joy and fulfillment that comes from walking more lightly on the earth. Studies on how the development of human values has progressed from those subsumed with self-centeredness and individualistic desires to those inspired by the shared oneness of the commonwealth of life will be useful to understanding better how this new concept of freedom can take hold.

In examining the impact of current human activity from an ethical perspective, the damage that has already been done by an economy too big for spaceship earth must also be taken into account. Although not all harm already done can be repaired, a moral economy must undertake restitution. That economy would have to be structured to allocate a sufficient share of its resources to deal with restoring stable populations of threatened and endangered species, to address the legacy of hazardous (toxic or nuclear) wastes, to revive destroyed habitat (forests, coral reefs, and the like), to mitigate the impacts of climate change, and to begin compensating for other impacts of past human economic activity. The economic activity required for restitution must be accounted for in establishing the scale limits required to set the economy in right relationship with our biosphere.

Discussion of the ethical prong of the I=f(PATE) framework leads naturally into the next chapter. It looks at how, once the impact of the human economy is scaled so as to maintain the integrity, resilience, and beauty of the commonwealth of life, its benefits and burdens can be fairly distributed.

What's Fair?
Sharing Life's Bounty

Love your neighbor as yourself.

—Leviticus 19:18, Mark 12:31

IMAGINE A BUSY CITY emergency room, around rush hour, suddenly overwhelmed by the victims of a mass transit accident. People with partially severed limbs, severe head wounds, out-of-control bleeding, and so forth are being rushed into the hospital admitting area on gurneys, their wounds barely being staunched by paramedics and their cries of pain filling the air. Doctors and nurses stand at the ready and begin the procedure of triage, that is, separating patients according to the urgency of their conditions. But instead of rushing the head wounds or internal injury cases into the emergency room, they first allow an older woman with a slight nosebleed into the case room; once she's dealt with, they lavish attention on a family whose daughter has a bad flu, followed by a man who may have broken his arm earlier in the day. It goes on like this until the outcry from the severely wounded is so disruptive that a few nurses, reluctantly, go over and began to treat some of the sufferers. Many are already dying.

In any emergency room, triage is applied because many people have arrived in need of medical attention, but medical supplies and personnel are in limited supply. Normally, the people in the most dire need of help take priority; the others wait in line. Heart attacks take precedence over bad cuts, and so forth. Triage is designed to save the greatest number of people possible. The way the benefits and burdens of today's global economy are distributed flips triage on its head—those who need the least get the most. They step to the head of the line, and the people and other species in the most dire need are left to suffer and to die.

Our current economy is geared to promoting as much short-term wealth and consumption as possible and to making sure that investments (the process of money making more money) increase as rapidly as possible, while minimizing regulation. As a result, the wealth divide between the superrich and the very poor, as well as between the average worker and their own CEO, keeps getting wider. That's just on the human level. For the commonwealth of life, one species among millions keeps stealing from present and future generations of its own and all other species. Those needing the most urgent help—forest systems, soil biota, gorillas, sharks, or frogs, among innumerable more—become expendable, because they are not even admitted to the emergency room in the first place. In some parts of the world, such as the United States, the idea of distributing the benefits and burdens more equitably is often vilified as unfair to all the people working so hard to become very rich themselves someday. People's vision of their getting to the head of the triage line outstrips their worrying about the fact, or even acknowledging the fact, that millions of people are living without the most basic levels of security, or about the deteriorating condition of soil, air, or water that affects us all.

Right relationship requires a fair basis for distributing the economy's benefits and burdens. In the context developed by Albert Schweitzer and Aldo Leopold, detailed in Chapter 2, fairness requires that living beings and living systems receive the means by which they can flourish. The challenge is to ensure fair distribution among *all* members of life's commonwealth, while at the same time preserving opportunities for healthy competition and diversity. An economy in right relationship with humanity and the earth's life systems encloses the spark of competition within the engines of social and ecological cooperation. Different levels of material wealth are possible, indeed inevitable, as citizens of the world pursue various opportunities for living within the earth's ecological limits. But fresh criteria are needed for distinguishing when these differences are a result of right or wrong relationship.

> *An economy in right relationship with humanity and the earth's life systems encloses the spark of competition within the engines of social and ecological cooperation.*

Rethinking Human Rights

Happily, the news is not all bad. Following the end of World War II, the idea of human rights gained global ascendancy, and culminated in the Universal Declaration of Human Rights in 1948.[1] The traditional distinctions between persons fade in the face of the evolution of this universal commitment to human rights. Although they were once paramount and still exist, especially on an emotional level, national identity, ethnic identity ("race"), and ancestral heritage are receding as requirements for basic moral entitlements. Today, nearly all nations of the world have begun to accept a universal duty to protect and enhance the basic rights of all other humans. In some regions of the earth—most of the twenty-seven nations in the European Union, for example, with its 500 million citizens— basic human rights are for the most part adequately protected, and the bulk of the population in those places, even the poor, are guaranteed adequate subsistence and health protections.

That other places still suffer a lack of human rights does not diminish people's increasing desire to act ethically. Global outrage erupts when the United Nations or various powerful countries do not step in to control gross human rights abuses in places like Zimbabwe, Sudan, China, or Burma. The international condemnation of the United States' overreaction and abuses following the

September 11 attacks and in connection with the Iraq War are a typical current reflection of the international recognition of human rights. This ethical progress shows the moral potential of humanity to include all of at least our own species within the umbrella of political and social concern. Yet just as a moral consensus may be emerging, it is essential to acknowledge that the very idea of human rights, and along with it the concept of distributive justice, must be rethought.

The rights and responsibilities set out in many national constitutions would take on radically different meanings if they were juxtaposed with a photo of the shrinking Arctic ice cap. There, the quick-moving effects of global warming graphically illustrate how political and moral choices as well as behavior interact with the earth's geophysical limits. At present, the American ideal of individual liberty is being spread around the world. Along with it, tragically, comes the desire for American levels of individual consumption. Combined with the increasing human population, this trend will substantially further destabilize the biosphere, resulting in vast numbers of plant and animal species going extinct, extreme disruption of the nitrogen and other natural cycles, and eventually catastrophic climate change.

The consequences of these changes are already bringing increased coastal flooding to low-lying areas of Asia, killing and driving from their homes people who are already living truly at the margins of survival. This is just the beginning, for the displacement of tens of millions of persons is already certain, given projections of continued global warming and the attendant sea-level rise that is already ensured by current atmospheric concentrations. John Rawls, perhaps the English-speaking world's leading figure in social and political philosophy in the last century, defines human rights as follows: "Each person is to have an equal right to the most extensive total system of equal basic liberties compatible with a similar system of liberty for all."[2] Rawls's precept of respect for others is one of the basic tenets of the whole idea of human rights. The morning traffic jams in Paris, Beijing, New York, and Mexico City are not merely inconveniences to motorists and people living near the highways, they are massive, systematic assaults on rights of other persons, both in those regions and throughout the globe. These unassailable facts have not sufficiently penetrated our society's collective conscience. Yet once we connect the idea of human rights with the laws of thermodynamics, as discussed in Chapter 2, and recognize that the earth is a spaceship, our understanding of those rights is altered profoundly and irrevocably.

Fairness to Whom?

Most Western ethical systems, such as those derived from the Judeo-Christian tradition and from ancient Greece, assume that issues of fair distribution concern shares of contested goods and services among persons pursuing a good and virtuous life. Accordingly, these ethical systems are concerned with how much income, wealth, medical care, offices carrying power and prestige, and so on each person is entitled to. The idea that other species could make claims for their fair share finds little, if any, footing in these traditions. Humans now use nearly half of all the ability of land-based plant life on the earth to convert sunlight into food and make it available to the web of life. When we also consider the ability to break down waste, human beings not only are overwhelming the ability of the biosphere to absorb carbon, but are also disrupting the phosphorous and nitrogen budgets and are threatening or destroying life in many aquatic systems.

As mentioned earlier in this book, according to studies that have attempted to assess the overall human ecological impact, such as ecological footprint measures,[3] the accelerating human impact is estimated already to be exceeding the capacity of life systems to regenerate. Distribution in a whole earth economy based on right relationship does not consider shares solely among persons. Instead, right relationship requires developing the means for noticing when growth has gone too far—as, for example, when more and more life forms start being extinguished from planet Earth. In a whole earth economy, we humans will no longer ignore the inchoate claims of other species for, literally, their place in the sun, but will recognize that equity among humans, equity between humans and other species, and inter-generational equity are all essential to preserving the resilience, integrity, and beauty of life's commonwealth.

In a whole earth economy, humans will no longer ignore the inchoate claims of other species for their place in the sun.

What Is Being Distributed?

The basic good for distribution that makes all other goods possible is the ability to harness energy, mostly from sunlight, to create and sustain life. Each share of this good (called net primary productivity, or NPP) is ultimately built on plants' ability to convert sunlight into molecules that can be broken down by other organisms to support their own ability to create and sustain life. Much of human history can be regarded as a quest for these life-giving molecules—the quest for dominion over forest, field, fisheries, and fossil fuels.[4] Each share also includes a proportion of the limited capacity of these life-building processes to assimilate all the products of material transformation and then complete (and hence restart) the cycle of consumption and reuse. With human domination of the globe now nearly complete, this process of harvesting the products of sunlight is reaching an endgame. The quest for cheap fuel and other resources that keep the economy's engines churning is spurring serious conflicts among human societies; and the human economy is demanding more and more shares of plants' ability to create these molecules.

Money allows humans access to the limited capacity of the earth's life systems to produce what humans and other members of life's commonwealth consume, and to assimilate what is left over.

Yet monetary systems are tied directly to the predominant world economic order, and therefore fail to recognize ecological limits. We might take a minute to think about money as a license to use up some of the shares of the earth's limited capacity to create and sustain life. Why should some people have more shares than others? How many shares does it make sense to give someone who has mastered the stock market, or gotten lucky at poker? And why should we humans, as a species, have all the shares, or even as many as we already have? Just as an economy in right relationship with the earth must be seen as embedded in the ecosphere, a new way of accounting is needed that reflects the limited amount of net primary productivity that can be used by humans and other species before exceeding—as we already do—the rate at which regeneration is possible.

Providing for Present and Future Generations of Life's Commonwealth

The clear trajectory of mainstream economics is to legitimate and expand the American ethic of distribution—the system of reverse triage that up until now really has not been overwhelmingly accepted on this planet. One reason that Africa is subject to mass famines, for example, is that in cultures on that continent many people will share until there actually is no food left, and then many starve together. In numerous traditional rural societies, there has been much less of the rich strolling past the starving on their way to a fancy restaurant, common in the West. The competitive economic ethic that underlies the world's major economies and their institutions will further undercut the already precarious existence of hundreds of millions of the world's most vulnerable people, whose ethics of sharing provides some protection (or used to do so).

This is simply to say that in the current era, our already limited conception of distributive justice is even further eroded as indiscriminate economic growth has become increasingly established as the public religion. Economic theory for about a hundred years has remained largely indifferent to questions about poverty, fair distribution, and justice, assuming that "rational actors" in a market economy, being equipped with perfect knowledge about all the impacts of their economic actions, will automatically make the best choices.[5] Some economists with strong market-fundamentalist tendencies, together with their political and corporate elite allies, claim that human goals are most reliably expressed through maximizing the market value of production. Prevailing economic theory fails to focus adequately on who bears the costs and reaps the benefits of such maximization, or how it generates poverty in one place even as it promotes excessive material abundance in another. This has further allowed market fundamentalists to promote the idea that maximizing production's market value is synonymous with maximizing human welfare, something that standard theory does not claim or prove and that daily experience is certainly far from bearing out.

Not even the planet's collective future lies beyond the reach of these impoverished doctrines. The blind faith in the market that underlies much of our political and social behavior conveniently undervalues the future in many of its calculations. In virtually all economic accounting systems used today, future events, whether favorable or unfavorable, have less importance than those that occur in the present. Discounting in this manner is full of mischief— mischief, as discussed below, that is perhaps fatal to civilization.

To ensure adequate consideration of future generations, the general practice in cost benefit analysis, which discounts the value of future needs, should be reexamined. Under the current economic system, only current uses and desires are granted full value. For example, the U.S. National Oceanic and Atmospheric Administration uses discount rates to determine its projects' costs and benefits.[6] To explain how it uses discounting, NOAA gives the example of a salmon habitat restoration project that will produce salmon valued at $10 million in ten years (NOAA calls this the salmon's "catch value"). Discounted at 3 percent, the present value of the salmon in year ten is about $7.4 million. Discounted at 10 percent, it is about $3.9 million. If the project costs $5 million, using a discount rate and choosing its value is critical, because it can determine whether the project will be built. In this example, using no discount rate means fully valuing now, at $10 million, the salmon that will exist in ten years, thus creating the strongest justification for funding the habitat restoration project.

Discounting virtually ensures that current generations will not leave a reserve of nonrenewable resources, or a reserve of the earth's bioproductive and bioassimilative capacity, for the use of future populations of humans as well as other species. In thinking about issues like averting climate change—where the costs occur in the present, and the benefits in the remote future—the idea of discounting implicitly provides an excuse to do little to protect the well-being of future generations of human and other life.

One justification for discounting the future that mainstream economists make is that a nonrenewable resource in use today will be substituted by "an abundant resource" that will eventually be made accessible after technological advances. If conventional oil runs out, for example, it will be replaced by liquefied coal or "heavy" oil from tar sands. As the price rises, it is assumed that the market will find its way around scarcity. Conveniently ignored are the millions of other species on the earth. Far too often, new technologies designed to provide access to these replacement resources require vast changes to the earth's surface. Think of coal mining in Appalachia that requires that whole mountaintops be blasted away, or the tar-sands mining that rips up the entire forest and wetland ecosystem and leaves a moonscape. Tearing up the earth is only one extraction method. Other methods are the diversion of already scarce water from use by humans or wildlife—as in vast quantities of the Athabaska River now going into the tar-sands settling ponds; inland water being diverted from the once-vast Aral Sea, in central Asia, to feed short-term industrial agriculture; and the Aswan Dam undercutting the Nile Valley's soil fertility. Add to this the emission of gases from vehicles and machines worldwide, causing acid rain and global warming, which accompanies any sort of building, extraction, or industrial intervention. Finally, the new, supposedly greener technologies simply might not materialize. Substitution and technical innovation should be encouraged when practical, but only within the context of our duties to life's commonwealth, and only on the basis of honest information and careful, realistic assessments of potentially available technologies.

What's Fair?

Once a new conception is adopted of the goods to be distributed and of the claimants entitled to participate in their fair distribution, criteria are needed to ensure that the distribution of both the benefits and the burdens of the economy is indeed fair and moral. In a whole earth economy based on right relationship, with an expanded view of distributive justice, any use or distribution of resources that impairs the ability of life to flourish in its full diversity would be immoral. Of course, all of life, human life included, depends on consuming other life. This mutual dependence is part of what it means to be a commonwealth. All species have enemies—some the size of tigers, others the size of microbes—that they seek to elude or destroy. This is an essential feature of the struggle of existence and reproduction. Right relationship does not deny these facts but only asks, as Albert Schweitzer and many aboriginal cultures remind us, that we act with respect and compassion toward others.

Right relationship only asks, as Albert Schweitzer and many aboriginal cultures remind us, that we act with respect and compassion toward others.

Already, human use of resources that threatens other species with extinction or with severely compromised numbers is generally considered immoral, and is even illegal in many countries. Taking this kind of moral principle to its logical extension, human society in a whole earth economy would realize, deep in their hearts and skin, that respecting other species' right to flourish promotes a healthy biosphere, and that in turn enhances the well-being of humans now and in the future. A fair distribution among present and future generations of the human and nonhuman community will be supportive for humans, but has the added dimension of permitting life's full commonwealth to flourish.

Think back to the $I=f(PATE)$ framework presented in Chapter 3. As discussed there, if the I variable, human environmental impact, becomes too big, the earth's natural systems are drawn down faster than they can regenerate. This limit on impact (I) accounts for the fact that shares must be provided to other species, which have their own I factors, as well as for present and future generations of all species. The first step, then, is to establish the total impact (I) share that is available for humans. This task has been described in previous chapters. It involves ensuring that enough bioproductivity is left for other species to thrive and that materials from human economic activity, such as heavy metals, greenhouse gases, or other pollutants, do not accumulate in the ecosphere. Once measures have been put in place to assess the efficacy of efforts to aid rather than destroy natural systems, to be described in Chapter 5, natural systems will begin to recover. In short, sharing with other life forms is what will enable humans to thrive in reasonable numbers, and once they realize that, the needed legislation and institutions to protect the biosphere will likely be increasingly supported by human societies.

The devil is always in the details, of course. Once the total impact (I) share available to all humans is established, the average per capita human share will depend on the total human population, along with the A, E, and T variables, that is, how lightly technology allows people to use the earth's bounty. Ecological footprinting is one way—still in need of further study and refinement—to establish these limits and shares through a standardized but, possibly, flexible measure.

It is unlikely, and indeed probably undesirable, that all humans be limited to an equal per capita share. Moral criteria are needed to determine what kind of variation is acceptable, especially for distribution among humans. If the economy exists for sustaining life, then any distribution that fails to supply the subsistence needs of any subset of the global population is an unfair, immoral distribution. Morality therefore requires redistribution from excess accumulation of material wealth to those who have less than they need. There will have to be global taxation. Global taxes will reach even the distribution-allergic United States. Fair wealth distribution also requires that the economy's burdens be redistributed. The concept of environmental justice, for example, is that no segment of the human community should suffer disproportionately from the effects of pollution, toxic waste, and climate change. That means that the practices of locating dumps, incinerators, nuclear waste storage depots, heavy industry, and so forth in poor, rural, or otherwise marginal areas would become illegal, with heavy penalties. If those living in affluent areas were forced to deal with society's wastes, the impetus would be provided to use optimal disposal methods or, better yet, to eliminate dangerous wastes altogether. This is another arena in which the EU shows leadership.

The provision of basic human needs for *all* the world's people is the beginning of a fair distribution of the economy's benefits and burdens among people. Beyond provisioning for basic necessities, greater equality in general enhances the quality of life within the human community by increasing morale, providing a sense of belonging, and creating greater opportunities for interaction and dialogue. Societies with greater equality generally have much lower crime rates than those with less equality. Prisons and other security and anticrime measures use enormous resources that could be applied to far more

> *The provision of basic human needs for all the world's people is the beginning of a fair distribution of the economy's benefits and burdens among people.*

positive uses. In many respects, greater equality among humans can be viewed as a cornerstone of social cohesion and the integrity of individuals and communities alike, and can be instrumental in supporting, or reaching toward, a world built on right relationship.

The essential role of diversity in preserving the integrity, resilience, and beauty of life's commonwealth acts as a counterweight to the moral imperative for equality. For humans, diversity means that different spirits, endowed with different talents and inspired in different ways, will engage in the myriad forms of human endeavor and industriousness on which human society and happiness depends. Diversity is an engine of the human culture. Naturally, different human pursuits will reap divergent rewards and unequal levels of material wealth. But, in view of the dreadfully unjust poverty in the world today, right relationship requires urgent and massive redistribution.

One of the principal arguments against redistribution is the claim that it undercuts economic efficiency—the economy's ability to produce goods and services that people want at the lowest price. Not true, according to economic theory, which provides that a significant portion of income and wealth disparity has little to do with economic efficiency. Much of current income and wealth distribution is shaped and determined by institutions, structures, and endowments that have nothing to do with contribution to current output. Among these are genetic inheritance; social connections; clan or class structures; cultural attitudes toward gender, race, and class; institutional power structures; historical imperialism; slavery; financial speculation; and, finally, age-old custom. Also playing an important role are changing interpretations and conceptions of intellectual property that pass the benefits of one generation's creativity to the next. According to standard economic theory, income and wealth disparities that result from forces external to the market can be eliminated through redistribution with no loss of incentive and no shrinkage of the economic pie. On this point at least, economic theory aligns with right relationship in seeking fair distribution.

Governance:
New Ways to Stay in
Bounds and Play Fair

We are called to be architects of the future, not its victims.

—Buckminster Fuller

IN JUNE 2008, the Standing Committee on International Trade of Canada's House of Commons held a little-noticed, hastily convened hearing on a pending free trade agreement between that nation and Colombia. The witnesses included two labor experts from the Canadian Labour Council, an environmental expert formerly with the North American Commission for Environmental Cooperation, and two representatives of Canada Pork International, an agency devoted to promoting exports from the Canadian pork industry. The committee members from the party in government, which had negotiated the agreement, pressed the point that Canada had better quickly get the trade treaty in place, lest the United States or other countries beat them to it and take market share away from Canadian exporters and investors aiming to get a toehold in Colombia. When witnesses offered by the opposition parties testified about the more than 2,000 union activists killed in Colombia in the past twenty years with alleged involvement of the police and military, the government party members said things were getting better and the trade agreement would help even more. Committee members grilled the pork industry representatives on how many more pigs they would sell, for how much more money, and with how many Canadian jobs created, if the agreement were approved. But no committee member asked about the amount of additional pig wastes to be added to Canadian air, soil, and water, or how much more greenhouse gases would be produced by shipping more pork to Colombia, let alone what overcrowding, antibiotics, and other routine matters of large-scale pork production were doing to the pigs' own well-being.

Concerns about the agreement's labor and environmental impacts came out through questioning the expert witnesses. For example, the agreement allows private investors to seek multimillion-dollar awards if they think the Canadian or Colombian government has violated the agreement by expropriating their investment or treating them unfairly. In pathetic contrast, it only allows a civil society group concerned that the few environmental provisions are not being obeyed to send a question to a bureaucrat and hope for an answer. Although the committee entertained more robust provisions, the hearing left little hope that anything would be done to improve the agreement's weak environmental and labor provisions. In fact, the hearing began with an announcement that the government had gone ahead and signed the agreement—without even waiting for the hearing to take place.

Take out Canada and Colombia from this example and insert any number of other countries—the United States or the European Union for Canada, and pretty much any Latin American or Asian country for Colombia—and you will have a picture of how free-trade deals are moving forward in much of the world these days. In trade and many other matters, governments virtually always assume that their national interest is identical with the economic goals of the industries or business interests that stand to profit from the trade agreement, because, it is thought, these interests will serve the supreme goal of adding to economic growth, hence a happy government and a contented populace. The only input for the effects of industry on labor and the integrity of natural systems are a few toothless provisions[1] that are only included because it would be politically touchy not to be able to at least refer to them, like a lucky touchstone.

These trade deals illustrate perfectly how the nations of the world are governing the global economy. Governance is the use of authority and resources to manage society's problems and affairs. New thinking is needed that breaks away from the prevailing limited conception of what is in the local, national, or global interest, and needed quickly, so as to create the kind of institutions and governance required first to restore and then to enable life's flourishing. To pave the way for alternative governance models, it is useful to analyze why the present models are not working. Governance is not just for government bureaucrats, politicians, and policy wonks. Right relationship for governance embodies the notion that, properly construed, government is not an "other," to be opposed and vilified, but rather a representation of collective wisdom, spirit, and discipline. It is something in which each of us as a citizen of the world has not merely a stake but a duty to participate.

> *Right relationship for governance is something in which each of us as a citizen of the world has not merely a stake but a duty to participate.*

The example of the United States helps explain why we need new approaches to governance. The United States is a country that issues inspiring statements of policy about the environment and has a full panoply of environmental laws. The national environmental policy of the United States, adopted in 1970 and still in effect, recognizes the need "to maintain conditions under which man and nature can exist in productive harmony, and fulfill the social, economic and other requirements of present and future generations of Americans."[2] Following this visionary, albeit anthropocentric, commitment the United States adopted the Clean Air Act and the Clean Water Act, which established regulatory, enforceable limits on the amount of pollutants that can be emitted to air and water. Then came the powerful Endangered Species Act, which has on numerous occasions stopped development in its tracks through effective enforcement. Other laws followed, such as laws regulating the handling, shipment, disposal, and cleanup of hazardous wastes, toxic substances, and pesticides.

At various times, state or federal administrations have sought to weaken these laws or their implementation, as with resistance by the federal government to use its authority to control greenhouse gas emissions. And, despite these laws, many signs point to the fact that several recent administrations have been far from stalwart defenders of the environment on issues such as protection of wildlife, coal mining, and climate change, among myriad others. But by and large these laws have led to some significant environmental improvement over the past forty years.

A strong and independent court system has played a crucial role in the credible enforcement of these laws, giving them real deterrent impact, though the courts' zeal has been progressively imperiled by a move to the right. For all the recent talk of voluntary compliance and market mechanisms, the backbone of environmental protection in the United States continues to be command-and-control regulation, in which the government sets and enforces strict environmental limits. Few people are seriously promoting the idea that this command-and-control system be dismantled. More recent regulatory schemes that incorporate market mechanisms, such as cap and trade systems, have had some success, particularly with acid rain, but they have at their root enforceable limits—the "cap" part of cap and trade. What has worked so far to protect the environment in the United States is command-and-control regulation with teeth, not laissez-faire capitalism.

Even with the finances and an intermittent will to protect, as well as the regulatory power, why then is the average per capita ecological footprint in the United States 23.7 acres, or 9.6 hectares (2003 data), when the world average is less than one quarter of that, at 5.4 acres, or 2.2 hectares? The global per capita footprint that would allow for strong resilience is something less than 4.4 acres, or 1.8 hectares (an area per person that would, in fact, leave nothing to other species).[3] Why is the United States a global laggard in addressing climate change? Why does it still countenance serious environmental problems, such as smoggy cities and innumerable waterways that fail to meet limits on mercury and other substances, making them unfishable and unsafe to swim in?

Why Governance Is Not Working

Constructing a society that favors instead of destroys life will require a rethinking of governance in line with right relationship with life's commonwealth on this dynamic but finite planet. Here is why.

The Inadequacy of National Governments

The first set of governance problems pertains to governance within the countries of the world. They are not addressing the earth's ecological crisis, for several reasons.

Velocity and Scale   Most countries designed their governance institutions in an era when the size of their human population and their economy were markedly smaller than they are today and when the environmental devastation they caused was considered local—if it was considered at all. At the time, changes in the earth's systems at the global level were slow. Today, vast and rapidly growing trends are changing the fundamentals of the earth's life-support systems. Even though several nations have developed complex environmental laws and policies, national governments by and large have failed to adopt systems of governance adequate to keep pace.

Failed or Failing States   A number of countries are so embroiled in civil wars, or their governments are so dysfunctional, that they cannot effectively establish systems to ensure adequate care of usual governance requirements such as security, taxation, or infrastructure, let alone new environmental responsibilities.

Capture In other countries, elites or special interests exert profound influence over the government, and they succeed in preventing adoption of effective environmental or financial controls that would threaten their economic interests. For example, the Clean Water Act in the United States, effective in 1972, contains weak provisions regarding certain kinds of water pollution, such as agricultural and urban runoff and certain kinds of pollution that falls as precipitate in rain from air emissions, like mercury and other heavy metals. Powerful agriculture, coal-mining, and electric utility lobbies help explain why.

Many Nations, One World Even if more national governments were proactive about the environment, their governance systems are inadequate to address global problems because many ecological threats do not recognize national boundaries. The most obvious and pressing example is climate change. Yet global warming is just one symptom of massive failure. A much larger, related crisis looms behind it: the oversized and growing global human appropriation of the products of photosynthesis (what we call our "ecological footprint"). Vast regional air pollution covers large swaths of Asia. Montreal has smog alerts aggravated by coal-fired power plants hundreds of miles away in the Ohio Valley of the United States.

Even the most developed governance systems have not been able to control their citizens' ecological impact. The top tier countries in terms of ecological footprint, with per capita footprints far in excess of their fair share, are the United States, the United Arab Emirates, Canada, Australia, New Zealand, and the Scandinavian countries.[4] Thus, the exorbitant ecological damage attributable to consumption in rich nations is often exacted in poorer ones. The fact, for example, that the United States has a huge, seemingly perpetual trade deficit means that it is a net exporter of its ecological footprint. The term "emerging markets," so loved by Wall Street and other investment communities, is often code for places with nonexistent, lax, or easily corrupted regulations on pollution and the exploitation of forests, fisheries, and labor. These are places where the regrettably named "human capital" and "natural capital" are to be had for the taking. Within nations these are de jure or de facto open-access systems where the rule is private appropriation of the benefits and externalization of the costs.

A major shortcoming of existing governance arrangements is that awareness of the urgency of growing global ecological threats has not triggered the voluntary agreement of nations necessary to make progress toward an economy in right relationship with life's commonwealth. The United States and China, for example, are major contributors to global climate change, with significant consequences for all nations, and yet neither is being held accountable to any international body for its behavior.

> *Awareness of urgent, global ecological threats has not triggered the voluntary agreement of nations necessary to make progress toward an economy in right relationship with life's commonwealth.*

Nickel and Diming In most countries, the environment takes a back seat to the economy. Government institutions in the United States have allowed its laudatory commitment to long-term environmental quality to be compromised in bits and pieces. The fine print of laws and regulations gives more weight to short-term economic impacts than to long-term environmental impacts. And the core principle of ecological resilience is not as easily applied to global ecological challenges, such as global warming and mass extinctions, that are less visible and appear less immediate than conventional pollution problems, even if they are more ominous.[5]

The Devil Is in the (Boring) Details Because these broad, looming ecological challenges are most clearly apparent at an aggregate scale, addressing them requires the time- and resource-consuming collection of huge amounts of data and information. Government programs in the United States that are devised to analyze such large pictures are often poorly designed or implemented. For example, the U.S. Clean Water Act requires the government to develop total maximum daily loads (TMDLs) of pollution for degraded water bodies. TMDLs are designed to restore water to healthy conditions and serve as a planning tool to apportion the allowable pollutant load among all known sources, both natural and human-derived. The concept is sound, but just as with the global system for apportioning the right to emit greenhouse gases, developing and implementing TMDLs has been extremely slow.

The Failure of International Governance Regimes

The present system of sovereign national governments dates from the Peace of Westphalia, two treaties signed in Germany in 1648 that curtailed a long cycle of territorial wars in Europe and created mutually recognized sovereign nation states. Today, sovereign countries the world over that mutually recognize each others' sovereignty interact through diplomatic channels as well as through organizations like the United Nations. Mutual recognition of sovereignty, backed up now with international law regimes that most countries accept, provides an important though very imperfect bulwark against war and conflict. But the system of sovereign states is not up to the challenges of our era. Here is why.

No Means to Ensure Fairness Not a single international institution exists to guarantee even a minimum standard of sharing in the earth's bounty. For both humans and nonhumans alike, the situation is simply grotesque. In a world awash in money, there are hundreds of millions of people, or by many measures billions of people, who lack the means to acquire even minimal goods such as clean water, shelter, food, preventive medical care, and the like. For nonhumans the situation is even more dire—the question of their fair share hardly arises at all, and more and more are dying off. And even when it does arise there is no effective mechanism to stop the precipitous decline in life's variety.

Growth Über Alles Institutions like the United Nations (UN), the World Trade Organization (WTO), the World Bank, the International Monetary Fund (IMF), and the International Labor

Organization (ILO) have opened the door to better ecological governance. They all have, to one degree or another, programs and rules that promote consideration of environmental and social impacts of the work they do, and most have adopted various accountability mechanisms that allow the public to raise environmental and social concerns.

But when was the last time you heard a government official or a person in the media applaud higher energy prices, because they will lead to more conservation and less greenhouse gas emissions and other ecological impacts? Almost always, the immediate promise of politicians is to make every effort to drive the prices down again. Even though the growth-oriented laissez-faire approach is directly correlated with ecological degradation and its social consequences, most nations fear short-term damage to their economies and a backlash from the financial interests that support them, so they fail to work on supplying sufficient protections for life's commonwealth. Hence, environmental and social safety net provisions are nearly always secondary, with development and growth the driving priority.

The international community has had little serious discussion that could lead to an understanding that global economic institutions are embedded in the biosphere on which they depend. As a consequence, when there is a clash between efforts to ensure living within the earth's ecological means and short-term economic growth, even the most dire ecological scenarios, like those in the increasingly foreboding reports of the International Panel on Climate Change, are insufficient to place effective checks on growth.

Power Imbalances   The governance arrangements reflected in today's international institutions are still biased toward the great powers reigning over the world when they were set up. The UN was founded at the end of World War II and is largely controlled by five countries with a veto power in the Security Council: the United States, Britain, France, China, and Russia—the main powerbrokers at the end of that war. Despite its shortcomings, the UN has been a decisive positive influence in the world on many issues, yet its more powerful members have not allowed it to be effective in addressing looming ecological crises.

The international business community has steadily used the World Bank, the WTO, and the IMF, all of which the United States has also dominated, to advance the goals of the economic model of unlimited growth and resource use. As in the example of the Canada–Colombia free trade agreement, economic interests that have the resources to exercise overt and covert control make sure to get involved in how these international institutions are run. The result: a world economy dominated by transnational companies and financial elites that operate with active support or passive acquiescence of national governments. Thus, though no effective global or international government exists, a de facto system of governance does exist, run by the economic interests that dominate the most powerful nations. The current system implicitly rejects, and for the most part would not seriously consider, governance options centered on respect for the earth's ecological limits and a fair distribution of its ecological capacity.

> *The current system implicitly rejects governance options centered on respect for the earth's ecological limits and a fair distribution of its ecological capacity.*

Little Power, Less Money The international institution at the global level that is most explicitly responsible for the environment is the UN Environment Programme. UNEP, though, lacks the authority and status of other global institutions, such as the WTO and the ILO. It is significantly underresourced and has no means of compelling right behavior. Proposals for global institutions for the environment were first made in the late nineteenth century, with more recent discussions dating from the 1970s onward.[6] Recent discussion focused on creating a World Environment Organization with enforcement powers similar to those of the ILO or WTO, and has also included various reform proposals of the intellectually rich but ineffectual UNEP.[7] However, despite many useful environmental programs at

UNEP and other UN agencies, an effective global environmental institution does not yet exist.

Talking but Not Walking   So far, the international community has at least paid lip service to the need to address the world's ecological and social crises. The 1948 Universal Declaration on Human Rights, the 1972 Stockholm and 1992 Rio Declarations that voiced a commitment to sustainable development, and the 2000 Millennium Development Goals, along with numerous programs of various UN agencies, the World Bank and other development banks, and the Global Environment Facility—all are, in theory, committed to improving the well-being of global society and protecting the environment for present and future generations. Several international mechanisms have actually been quite successful, most notably the Montreal Protocol on Substances that Deplete the Ozone Layer (signed originally in 1987), which has led to dramatic reductions in the release to the atmosphere of chemicals that destroy the ozone layer, despite the refusal of countries like China and India to join in.[8] But by and large, international institutions have not yet succeeded in translating those words into effective action that sets enforceable rules for preventing economic growth from undermining human and ecological well-being.

A Step in the Right Direction   At least one current international effort holds the promise to be a model, in part, for the greater effort that must follow. The International Panel on Climate Change, while certainly not immune to political intermeddling, has displayed admirable impartiality that provides a hopeful example. The IPCC has demonstrated a commitment to seeking honest information about climate change's causes and effects, with a view to driving international consensus on the action needed to address the climate change crisis. It has a decent degree of credibility and independence. It is incomplete, though, since it has not yet been linked to a reliable mechanism for building enforceable international rules that will respond to the information it is producing. Whether the IPCC is a successful model depends on whether this linkage occurs.

Principles of Governance in Right Relationship with Life's Commonwealth

Right relationship can be reflected in governance systems through a core set of principles that are essential to effective governance. These core principles relate to capacity and authority, credibility, accountability and effectiveness, transparency, and subsidiarity.

Capacity and Authority   Governance systems and procedures at the global, national, and subnational level must have, first, the capacity to establish ecological limits on economic activity and, second, the authority to set and enforce rules that will allow human and nonhuman life and the systems they rely on to flourish for generations to come. This implies the authority to foster freedom of individual economic choice as much as possible, but within spheres limited as necessary to protect the commonwealth of life.

Credibility   Government institutions and systems of governance need to have their constituents' confidence in order to enact, implement, and enforce regulatory systems and procedures and to govern on behalf of humanity and life's commonwealth. This requires that they rely on honest sources of information and be independent from corrupting influences.

Accountability and Effectiveness   Government institutions need to be held responsible for their policies and behavior, which must be measured in honest, open ways against preestablished goals and criteria. They must be prepared to make adjustments when they fall short, so that institutions or government actors that do not perform can be replaced with ones that do.

Transparency   Government-held information must be freely available, to enable fair assessments of a government's performance and hold its institutions accountable.

Subsidiarity   Governance institutions should be as local as possible. They should be built around ecosystems instead of artificial political boundaries. People should be meaningfully consulted about policies that affect them locally, and local governments should possess authority to apply broadly applicable rules setting limits that best fit the local culture and ecology. Acting locally in self-interest has limits, though. Local actions and behavior often affect other neighborhoods, the local environment and quality of life are affected by outside activities, and local government is prone to capture just as national governments are. At all levels of government, rules are needed so that all actors respect collective limits that are necessary to ensure right relationship.

Introducing Four Proposed Global Institutions for a Whole Earth Economy

How should fair access to the earth's limited capacity to support and maintain life be governed? The functions missing at the global level are:

- The comprehensive monitoring and analysis of information on the ecological limits of the earth, in a way that can be applied to keep the economy within those limits (though bits and pieces of this kind of work do exist)
- Means to protect the global commons in a fair way
- A means of passing enforceable rules and regulations
- Independent judicial review of the performance of these institutions and compliance with global rules

The proposals below may not be the best solutions humanity can come up with for supplying the governance now missing at the global level, but they have been carefully considered and are offered here to help focus attention on the urgent tasks ahead. In any event, it is their functions, not what they are called, that are most important. A global discussion must begin on how to bring institutions resembling the four that follow into being in a democratic, participatory way that will avoid the political and economic traps that have so far compromised so much of national and international governance. They serve as functional ideals to which we must aspire, no matter what particular form they take. Such a task is, of course, an enormous challenge. But the first step of that challenge is to envision these institutions, and how they could bring effective governance to the commonwealth of life.

The first proposed institution is a *Global Reserve*, endowed with a well-supported research component, that would guide the economy based on the biophysical laws that govern the planet. This would also require an integrated understanding of the earth's economic/ecological household budget, that is, its real ability to use and renew the planet's finite resources. The Global Reserve would develop and update information on the dynamics of human ecological impact, the ways in which the benefits and burdens are being allocated and distributed, and the ecological limits that must bind the economy. Information from the Global Reserve would serve the other institutions.

The second institution would be *Trusteeships of Earth's Commons* to protect the ozone layer, the atmosphere, the oceans, and the other systems necessary for life's flourishing, by monitoring and administering the limits, allocations, and distributions deemed necessary through the work of the Global Reserve.

The third proposed institution is a *Global Federation*, modeled in part on the European Union, with jurisdiction over the operation of a whole earth economy and with the authority to adopt and administer binding international laws establishing limits and allocations on the human use of the earth's resources, and to ensure fairness among persons and between humans and other species. Critical to its success are government institutions at national and subnational levels that also respect these foundational principles. Properly designed, the Global Federation could sustain and enable, not stifle, the local traditions and natural wonders that give life meaning in particular places and ways, because these are the things that define various cultures and ecosystems and hence, in significant part, human identity and individuality. Last, a *Global Court* would be needed to resolve disputes arising out of the operation of these institutions and to hold them to their charters.

The Earth Charter, an international initiative launched in The Hague, Netherlands, in 2000, lays out a hopeful vision of what these institutions could accomplish.[9] The result of a civil society project led by Mikhail Gorbachev and Maurice Strong and with broad and diverse participation from around the world, the Earth Charter recognizes the need to maintain the economy within the earth's limits. It sets out principles in four categories: respect and care for the community of life; ecological integrity; social and economic justice; and democracy, nonviolence, and peace. Keeping the Earth Charter in mind will help in developing the right kind of global governance for a whole earth economy.[10]

The Global Reserve

The principal purpose of the Global Reserve is the analysis of the earth's life support budgets and their uses in accordance with right relationship with the commonwealth of life.

The first major global institution proposed is the Global Reserve. The World Bank and the International Monetary Fund must give way, either by rapid evolution or by replacement, to an institution charged with understanding how the economy works within the ecosphere. Thus, one of the central tasks of the Global Reserve will be to understand and develop a framework for managing life's commonwealth in accordance with the concept of right relationship. The Global Reserve will need vast scientific expertise in the fields of ecosystem function and restoration, along with the ability to frame appropriate issues for public consideration and official decision making. In short, it will need to have the power to deal with the tough moral questions that lie unaddressed now—but that, without action, will become ever more difficult over time.

Using the I=f(PATE) Framework

The Global Reserve should make good use of the I=f(PATE) framework discussed in Chapter 3, with the goal of preventing the total human economic impact from overrunning the integrity, resilience, and beauty of life's commonwealth. A compelling virtue of this framework is that it highlights the available arenas of policy and moral choice: Population, Affluence, Technology, and Ethics. Some tools are already available to assess the impacts of economic activity in line with the I=f(PATE) formula: Examples include assessment of the appropriation of net primary productivity, environmental impact assessment, state-of-the-environment reporting, assessment of carrying capacity, and estimates of how much remains of various resources like oil and how to do real risk assessment that considers the reality of ecosystem fragility. Other tools, such as measurements or indices of quality of life, population studies, ecological footprinting, climate change science, and so on, are also being rapidly elaborated. Ecological footprinting is perhaps the most developed attempt to assess overall human impact, as described in the I=f(PATE) formula, but it both understates *and* overstates impact and requires further study and refinement.[11] The capacity to do much of this work already exists in the United Nations agencies, the World Bank and other development banks, and related international institutions and organizations.

The Global Reserve would make use of these and similar tools to help define the limits that the biosphere puts on human economic activity, and to provide information to authorities, like the proposed Global Federation and the Trusteeships, that set rules or guidance to ensure that the economy stays within those bounds. Nation states or other subsidiary levels of government could also use information from the Global Reserve to decide how to adjust the variables in their particular I=f(PATE) framework, so as to stay within their fair allotment of the total global human impact (I). This idea is simply an extension of ideas growing out of the approach to controlling anthropogenic climate change. Each country has a target and can choose how to stay within it, subject to verification by the Global Reserve. As the Global Reserve becomes more operational, more targets, such as biodiversity conservation, pure-water availability, amount of forest cover, and so forth, could be added to the understanding of biosphere needs that would guide all four institutions.

Population   In making policy choices using the I=f(PATE) framework, the most challenging factor is likely to be population. In many countries, the I=f(PATE) framework will probably reveal that technological advances and reduction in consumption and waste are insufficient to ensure the integrity, resilience, and beauty of life's commonwealth. The prospect of population reduction and human settlement redistribution within the earth's ecological limits poses enormous ethical and practical difficulties. Will it be chaotic, tragic, and inequitable, or can it be accomplished in some orderly, cooperative, equitable way that honors life's commonwealth? To ask this question is to move into the zone of the almost unthinkable. Yet the Global Reserve must be prepared to develop the information that will frame the policy options for addressing population concerns.

Deciding on policies to reach a fair size for the human population and its consumption is an imperative early task for those in charge of managing the earth's ecological budget. By many accounts of interspecies equity, substantial population reductions, optimally voluntary and humane and resulting from decreased fertility rates, may become necessary. Much of the ecological harm done today is a result of flaws in the growth and development model now followed by nearly every national government. The countries that have achieved the most, as defined by that model—the industrialized economies of Europe, North America, Australia, and New Zealand in particular—do the most harm per capita. So it is here that reducing human numbers will pay the greatest ecological dividends. Of course, as other countries catch up (many of them are already recognized as being overpopulated), their problems will become even more urgent than they already are.

Consumption   In regard to affluence (consumption) and ethics in the I=f(PATE) framework, the honest and rigorous information that the Global Reserve collects on an ongoing basis to establish and refine ecological limits will need to counter the effect of advertising. The constant stream of advertising that bombards human society around the globe often uses deception, overstatement, and subconscious messaging to promote mindless overconsumption. Advertising too frequently transforms the amorphous and endless *desires* for luxuries, opportunity, and power that are a natural facet of the human imagination into *needs* that must be fulfilled right now.[12] Pandering to the childish and endlessly greedy side of human imagination creates a warped notion of what it means to be "happy." This is a manufactured manifestation of the "E" factor that has no basis in spiritual, ecological, or even practical material fulfillment. It also blocks out the moral doubt and consternation that people would otherwise feel when they consider that they may personally be demanding an unfair and excessive consumption of the earth's bounty. In a whole earth economy, the ability to choose between a broad array of earth-damaging products would no longer be considered real freedom. The Global Federation may need to enact legislation, or provide guidance to the nations and other subsidiary levels of governments to do so, that will confront the effects of deleterious advertising.

Advertisers could be required to follow any advertisement with a statement concerning the environmental impact or ecological footprint of the product being advertised, much like food processing companies are presently required to list nutritional information and drug companies are required to disclose side effects and sometimes "black box warnings." Germany has an admirable institution already doing this. Stiftung Warentest is a consumer guide service maintaining strict independence from both government and commercial interests.[13] Owing to its reputation for absolute integrity, it is consulted by some eight out of ten Germans before they purchase any goods, from vacuum cleaners to toothpaste. The consumer guides it publishes monthly assess products not just for durability and cost, but for the very effects on the biosphere that the Global Reserve would begin to make available. Its national moral and economic influence is so great that a poor rating—a vacuum cleaner that contains cadmium, for example, or wine bottles that cannot be recycled—pretty much dooms that brand to failure, despite all the producers' advertisements to the contrary. The simple fact that small institutions of this nature already exist points to the clear possibility for their expansion, even to the global level.

The Global Reserve should also develop information on the impacts of generating credit. Just as limits used to be (and again can be) placed on commercial advertising, they should be considered for credit generation, particularly the predatory lending practices that cause not merely overconsumption but also periodic loss and suffering in even the richest countries, to say nothing of the poorest.

Durability and high quality in all sorts of goods can and should be emphasized once again. Public campaigns are already being developed that promote simplicity and try to shield people from the worst affects of consumerism, such as the "What Would Jesus Drive?" campaign of the Evangelical Environmental Network and *Creation Care* magazine.[14] These campaigns are already enlisting the support of civic and religious organizations, though as yet they have had limited success in trying to work with government and state agencies, except in Europe.

Technology The politically most expedient factor in the I=f(PATE) framework is the technology factor. Beginning (and often ending) this process by putting emphasis on technological solutions lets politicians avoid the complications of asking their constituents to make do with less or to have fewer children. In a world inhabited by almost 7 billion people, technology will have to play a critical role in moving toward a moral economy, but it should never be an excuse not to address population and consumption.

The Global Reserve should concentrate primarily on scientific measurements and social change while, at the same time, subjecting all suggested—but as yet undeveloped—technologies to a credible dose of truth-testing, especially when they are offered in order to justify rejection of ecologically preferred alternative technologies available in the short term.

The Global Reserve also needs to address the reality that much of the current incentive to develop and promote "green" and other technologies comes from their potential to make profits. Without publically created incentives, investment in research and development devoted to public goods not easily privatized, such as clean air, is likely to fall short. Regrettably, the current intellectual-property regime (meaning patents) has increasingly privatized the scientific knowledge base, such as the patenting of living organisms. The Global Reserve will need to manage its surveillance of technological developments so as to ensure that intellectual-property rights do not prevent promising technologies that are not profitable or cannot be easily commoditized from serving the common good. To this end, it will need to develop a broad-based research and development framework.

The Stabilization, Allocation, and Distribution Functions of the Global Reserve

In conjunction with analyzing the ecological boundaries of the economy, the Global Reserve would have functions geared toward determining the means for stabilizing human ecological impacts, allocating the authority to take resources from and put wastes back into the environment, and distributing this authority fairly among present and future generations of the earth's species. The idea of having stabilization, allocation, and distribution functions derives from the organization of public finance systems and monetary reserves that typically have these functions.[15]

Stabilization   The chief purpose of the stabilization function is to maintain the ecological impacts of the economy at levels that do not overwhelm ecosystems' ability to adapt. Change is the order of all things on the earth and in the universe, but the velocity and character of change influence life's prospects dramatically.[16] A critical task in fulfilling the stabilization function will be to provide a description of how the earth's life systems respond to change—in essence, their integrity and resilience. Like determining what quantity of nutrients from farming destroys the functioning of

> *Change is the order of all things on the earth and in the universe, but the velocity and character of change influence life's prospects dramatically.*

an ecosystem such as the Everglades, the stabilization function will involve monitoring and analyzing the interdependence of key variables that control how ecosystems behave and also how interdependent variables interact. One aspect of this will be to track long trends, to identify major threats to life's commonwealth, and to develop information that can enable a response to threats that will be consistent with a healthy human–earth relationship. Much of the work relevant to this function, such as the Millennium Ecosystem Assessment, is already being done and could be consolidated and reinforced.

In short, there will be a healthy reluctance to introduce manmade changes to an ecosystem of any kind, pending careful study; and existing declines will be carefully analyzed in terms of what may have caused them. This is the very essence of the precautionary principle that already is included in international statements of commitment like the 1992 Rio Declaration and often guides global organizations like the UNEP. The precautionary principle is a beginning step. It attempts to put the onus to prove that a new product, chemical, industry, or development is benign on those attempting to introduce it—instead of waiting until clear damage forces victims to seek redress that, in terms of ecological integrity, almost always comes too late.

Allocation The allocation function of the Global Reserve is to measure and devise policies for using the human share of the earth's capacity efficiently to produce the forms of plant and animal life that humans consume and also for monitoring the earth's capacity to assimilate wastes. One promising allocation tool is an International Clearing Union (ICU), as proposed in 1943 by John Maynard Keynes during the Bretton Woods talks that led to the creation of the World Bank and the IMF. Keynes proposed the ICU as a trade-stabilizing mechanism to ensure that creditor nations would not come to dominate debtor nations.[17] The ICU would issue its own currency, to be called the *bancor*, to serve as the exchange unit for international trade. The ICU would determine the trade exchange rates with the national currencies through the bancor, and monitor any trade imbalances that arose. Should any nation develop a net trade surplus, its bancor exchange rate would be adjusted accordingly to disfavor future trade imbalances. The exchange rate would also be adjusted to prevent countries from falling too far into debt. Instead, the subsequent Bretton Woods Agreement created the World Bank and the International Monetary Fund, which, as their missions were hijacked by international financial interests, have led many developing nations to sink further into debt under unserviceable loans.[18]

An updated version of the ICU would help ensure fair and equitable international trade that maintains the integrity, resilience, and beauty of the commonwealth of life. By adding an ecological component, bancors could become *ecors*. Credits or debits of ecors could be tied to a nation's management (or mismanagement) of its ecological capacity, including but not limited to national net primary productivity (NPP). Policies that result in a net decrease in ecological function for a nation (as measured, for example, by satellite ground-cover mapping and other sources) would result in corresponding charges in ecors, thus creating incentives against further ecological degradation. Likewise, efforts on the part of that nation to increase ecological functions through such activities as reforestation would result in a corresponding increase of that nation's purchasing power through ecor credits. A service fee in ecor exchange could generate a restoration fund for work in qualifying nations, provided that these nations agree to ecological policy reforms.[19] Implementing such ideas is not really so far away. In early 2008, France and Germany suggested that a tax be put on Canadian goods because Canada was not complying with the industrial adjustments necessary to meet Kyoto Protocol climate change targets, and therefore had an unfair economic advantage over products from countries that were. If such a thing as an ecor already existed, this economic advantage would be even easier to rectify, and the result would be not merely a more level economic playing field, but also the likely acceptance of binding greenhouse gas emissions targets by currently uncooperative countries like Canada.

Distribution   The main purpose of the distribution function is to develop the basis for determining a fair distribution of the economy's benefits and burdens among present and future generations of humans and other species. The human share can be fairly distributed only after excluding the shares that must be left to the rest of life's commonwealth. In regard to the human share, few steps have been taken recently to move the world toward greater income and wealth equality. The global community, through the Millennium Development Goals and many other international programs, has focused on poverty reduction, which is certainly essential, but has made no attempt to address excessive wealth and overconsumption. And while these programs have had some local success, within many nations across the globe the continued adherence to the neoliberal growth economy has resulted in systematic dismantling or reduction of social safety nets.

The distribution function will have to start with honest, scientific information on what is legitimately available for current human use, taking into account the biosphere's regenerative capacities. The objective then will be to establish distribution mechanisms that ensure that basic needs of all humans are met, while also allowing for the variations in material wealth that are inevitable as different people pursue different kinds of lives. Today, greed and wealth have no enforceable limits. No limit exists on how many billionaires the world will allow, or how affluent one person can become. Those charged with the distribution function will face the difficult task of imposing new limits that recognize the immorality of an economy giving—for whatever reason—too much of the earth's capacity for life to too few inhabitants.

Global redistribution is essential for reversing the current social tendency of exalting massive wealth and consumption. The global community should ensure that basic human needs are provided for, not as a matter of occasional charity but as a matter of continuous justice and right. Individuals have the right to what they need to sustain life. The ability to engage in the community, and contribute to and benefit from it, is a cornerstone of a just economy. At the same time, people have a duty to contribute to society. All this implies that society must organize its institutions in such a way that every individual is granted a fair share of society's resources, including the opportunity to contribute to the community in a capacity that enhances human dignity and self-worth.

> *The ability to engage in the community, and contribute to and benefit from it, is a cornerstone of a just economy.*

One promising idea is to replace hit-or-miss foreign assistance by a guaranteed, planet-wide citizen's income. In addition to being substantially fairer than the present gross inequalities, such a system should provide incentives to reduce the birth rate. Many studies indicate that it will do so, among other reasons because most poor people have large numbers of children to provide security, particularly in old age. Because of the harm already done to global systems, poverty alleviation must be accomplished by redistribution, not by growth—at least when growth increases ecological impact. Of course, because wealthy people have much greater ecological impact than poor people, incentives to keep birth rates low among wealthy populations is critical, as well.

Since those with little income are likely to spend all or most of it on consumption, it is imperative that such a system be connected with a robust global regulatory structure. This structure should orient consumption away from damaging technologies such as private cars that use fossil fuels, or air conditioners that (despite global bans on ozone-depleting chemicals) emit small amounts of such substances and use energy that contributes to global warming, to give only two examples.

An important task of the distribution function is to make market corrections. Markets are ill-equipped to deal with both tangible and intangible environmental goods and issues, if only because environmental goods are public goods. One person can breathe clean air, and clean air is still there for others to breathe. The same largely holds true for a multitude of other environmental goods, such as clean water, biodiversity, wilderness, and climate stability. Even mainstream economists expect governments to find a way to provide public goods, including environmental goods.

Measures of aggregate income and wealth should include environmental goods and their distribution. With this approach, wealth would include the utility that people derive from sunlight and from clean air, soil, and water, as well as the value that human beings place on wilderness. The economy would also account for ecosystem services: the air, soil, water, and biodiversity that healthy ecosystems preserve to enrich and sustain the planet. A proper understanding of the economy's essential burdens and benefits that are available for distribution would lead to alternatives to current resource extraction, production, or industrial practices that would preserve and protect life's commonwealth. Under this approach, renewable energy sources and materials would have higher value, and nonrenewable energy sources and materials would have lower value.

Capacity building is closely linked with the distribution function. Many countries and regions will need help integrating and implementing policies and programs that are centered on maintaining the integrity, resilience, and beauty of life's commonwealth. Existing mechanisms like the Global Environmental Fund, which promotes, funds, and helps implement environmental projects, can serve as a starting point, but need to be adjusted so that they recognize the ecological limits on growth and development. For example, the full slate of GEF projects that promote development of renewable energy in developing countries may be a step in the right direction.[20]

Trusteeships of Earth's Commons

The principal purpose of the planetary trust, or trusts, is to protect the earth's life-support systems and to ensure that these systems be used for the flourishing of life's commonwealth.

The role of the Trusteeships of Earth's Commons will be to translate the information on ecological limits developed in the Global Reserve into measures necessary to manage the global commons in a manner that respects the flourishing of life's commonwealth. Peter Barnes examined the concept of Commons Trusts in his book *Who Owns the Sky?* and has extended the usefulness of the idea of trusteeship in his *Capitalism 3.0*.[21] He argues in favor of setting up what he calls a "sky trust" in the United States as a way to respond to the burgeoning climate crisis. The function of the trust would be to protect and maintain the common resource of the sky, so that it continues to function to the benefit of all life. The trust would use mechanisms such as cap and trade, which would involve setting a regulatory cap on the total amount of pollution that can be emitted into the sky, conducting an auction among polluters to initially assign and control emission rights, and then allowing polluters to buy and sell emission rights according to market prices. The cap would decline rapidly and predictably, consistent with prevailing independent scientific information on the degree of emissions reduction needed to avoid ecological catastrophe.

Each person is legally defined as a co-owner of this common property resource—the atmosphere. Each person, corporation, or other entity who wishes to use this resource to dispose of waste has to pay rent to the owners. Anyone emitting carbon dioxide or other greenhouse gases to the atmosphere would have to buy a permit, with the price based on the number of tons released. Trading of permits would be allowed in a regulated market. The money would be paid into a fund administered by trustees who would be independent of corporations or government, which Barnes regards as too prone to short-term interests to take the necessary long-term view. Indeed, the independence of the trustees is essential.[22] The sky trustees would invest the money or distribute it in accordance with a formula. One possibility would be a payment to all citizens, though at first the proceeds would be better used to subsidize technologies and programs geared toward reducing greenhouse gas emissions, adapting to climate change, or mitigating other environmental problems. The main function of the trust would be to preserve the resource, rather than solve poverty or distributional issues.

Trusts like this make sense for global commons at the international level as well. There could be a single global trust or a set of them, or perhaps a series of national trusts each operating within a national cap, or a mixed system of trusts and other mechanisms. If an emission quota is allocated equally to all persons on the earth, then the "sky trust" could initially serve as one, but by no means the only, major engine of redistribution in favor of the world's poor. Current per capita use by the rich is far beyond any quota sufficient to avert disaster. So the trust or trusts can serve as their agent and buy their quota annually, directly or indirectly, from the poor. As the global emissions quota is lowered, the prices of permits would rise—thus encouraging the rich to reduce their use, while moving toward climate stability and poverty reduction at the same time.[23] For reasons given below, however, in the long run, proceeds from trustee activities should likely go into general revenues.

Notably, the use of cap and trade mechanisms in connection with trusteeships can be made consistent with the principle of subsidiarity, or keeping governance at the most local level possible. Cap and trade mechanisms establish an overall limit, but allow the market and other factors to determine how emissions shares, or whatever other share is being capped and traded, are distributed. Establishing a defensible cap through honest scientific inquiry ensures that freedom of economic choice does not lead to overconsumption that is unfair to other members of life's commonwealth.

The trusts would operate on behalf of the entire commonwealth of all life. The earth's commons are the property not only of all persons, but also of all living beings present and future. So, much of the proceeds belong to nonhuman species and systems. Trusts could restore land degraded by strip mining, reclaim wetlands, implement recovery plans for species threatened with extinction, replant forests, invest in "green" chemistry to reduce the flow of toxins into the environment, and retard desertification. There is no shortage of opportunities for trustee governance to help societies the world over to live more responsively and respectfully in securing life's prospects.

The atmosphere's ability to store limited amounts of carbon is not the only commons. There are radio and other electronic frequencies, the oceans, biodiversity, scientific knowledge, the earth's fresh water, and many more. A catchall trusteeship might even be established around the concept of the ecological footprint, in which a cap and trade system for asserting an ecological footprint would be administered through a trusteeship. This means that the revenue sources available to trusteeships would be multiple and could be used to support, in significant measure, the other elements of global governance.

The Global Federation

The principal purposes of the Global Federation are global security and the protection of human rights and life's commonwealth.

The Global Reserve and the Trusteeships for Life's Commons described above will need a formal framework that incorporates them into the international community. The Global Federation provides this link. The primary missions of the proposed Global Federation would be to maintain global security and to protect and enhance human and nonhuman rights—which would be understood in the context of all peoples' responsibilities to their fellow humans and to all of life's commonwealth. The Federation would establish a global constitution establishing the charters for itself and the other global institutions, built around the core principle of right relationship.

The Global Federation would have legislative and executive functions. It would attempt to facilitate the ability to sustain cultural values and norms and protect local ecosystems that give life meaning in particular places and ways. Such values have long defined human societies' varied expressions of themselves. Despite the need for world government, the Federation could not function in a purely top-down manner. A democratically based Parliament would have to establish an executive government accountable to all the people who participate and support it. This government would have to be clearly accountable to the Parliament and responsible for carrying out its democratically determined wishes.

Structure of the Global Federation

Political scientists have made a number of proposals and discussions about how to fix the current global governance system. Richard Falk and Andrew Strauss have proposed a popularly elected Global People's Assembly.[24] George Monbiot developed the idea of a global parliament in *The Age of Consent*.[25] Another model is global federalism as proposed by Myron Frankman in *World Democratic Federalism: Peace and Justice Indivisible*.[26]

The Federalism model is already being adopted in Europe— albeit with considerable controversy, some of it over the dominance of business interests over social and environmental ones.[27] In the European model, existing nations become similar to European nations in Europe or to states or provinces in the American, Australian, Canadian, Mexican, and other federal systems. Some of the func-

tions of current nation states would be "bumped up" to the level of
the world federation. These include obligations of military security
among the several states, as well as the creation of institutions to
manage the global commons according to a set of common principles. In general, however, the government functions should be as
close to the local as possible, so as to recognize and help preserve
the diversity of the world's cultures, while the global character of
the federation would further stimulate the global culture already
well under way. People could then become citizens of both local
communities and the earth at large.

Whatever the form of global federation, it will need a parliament or other governing body. The British Parliament is an example of a unitary authority,[28] where all government agencies are the
responsibility of one central authority. The system in the United
States is an example of shared responsibility between a legislative
branch, which writes the laws, and a separately elected executive
branch, which implements and (together with the judicial branch)
enforces them.[29] Parliaments can be made up entirely of directly
elected members, as in Britain, or a mix of directly elected members plus representatives from another directly elected body, as in
Switzerland.[30] Governments can be composed and led in different
ways, such as by a president or a prime minister.

The current European Union has legislative authority divided
between an elected Parliament and a Council composed of ministers
from each of the nations. The executive branch is the Commission,
headed by one commissioner from each of the 27 nations making
up the European Union. The model favored here would take the
current European model as a starting point, but would ensure that
only directly elected members are responsible for governance so
that they could remain accountable to local constituencies.

There is a considerable danger that a Global Federation would
be captured by the "empire of the day," just as the GATT (subse-
quently the World Trade Organization), the World Bank, and the
International Monetary Fund were subordinated to the United

States following World War II. In the design of a global parliament and government, great care must be taken to avoid having them become subordinate to particular nations or interests. One possible approach is to adopt strong charters or constitutions that establish clear, enforceable core principles that strictly limit the channels through which money can corrupt effective governance.

To oppose a Global Federation because it sounds like Orwell's "Big Brother"[31] is to allow actual control of the planet to remain in the hands of the current de facto Big Brother of unelected, unaccountable commercial leaders and entities that recognize no responsibility for the public good. Governance must be exercised at a global level for global issues, but must have local grounding to ensure relevance and accountability. In this regard, the principles for good governance listed earlier bear repeating in relation to this proposed Global Federation.

Subsidiarity means getting the balance right between global, national, and local levels. The purpose of establishing a global economic governance system is to control those aspects of the global economy that require minimal global standards to ensure fairness and adequate ecological safeguards. Indeed, this approach will help remove what is currently a perverse form of subsidiarity: the growing tendency of national or subnational governments to base local decisions on a perceived need to remain competitive internationally, in subservience to a trade and finance regime in which capital tends to seek the lowest level of labor, environmental, and other types of regulation.

Accountability and transparency can be ensured through a mixture of measures, including fair election of parliamentary members, public accessibility to knowledge of the activities of the organization (such as financial and other reports), freedom-of-information legislation, and regular auditing by different independent auditors. A number of countries use the office of an ombudsman or auditor general to assist with accountability and accessibility. Critical to transparency is the assurance that reviews and inspections are not compromised or deleted if responsibilities are contracted out or assigned to subsidiaries.

The ability of an organization to be in control of its revenue or income would be critical to its independence. The example of Stiftung Warentest given earlier, though small and local, is useful. It was initially founded with government funding, but quickly became independent of both government and business (which was never allowed any financial role) through the publication of its consumer guides and magazines. In short, the social community it serves also supports it financially, which is the best and safest arrangement for the economic independence of these institutions.

A Regulatory Role for the Global Federation

"The Tragedy of the Commons," a term coined by Garrett Hardin in a famous essay in 1968,[32] contends that without effective controls, people will overuse and destroy any public commons, such as the atmosphere or the oceans. The tragedy of the commons postulates that reliance on individual action to prevent overconsumption or to promote conservation at a sufficient level is almost certainly doomed to fail. Individual assessment of how much of a resource can be used generally does not account for ecological limits, which need to be defined at a collective scale. The proposal to address the tragedy of the commons through privatization has been controversial[33] and has often actually added to the problem of commons degradation. The other main alternative is public regulation, which can be applied with fewer concerns over how to fairly distribute property rights to use common resources.

A regulatory system requires several key elements, including a means for establishing regulatory limits that are deemed fair and effective, a feedback process for monitoring and continual adjustment of regulatory limits, a system for using incentives where regulations may stifle innovations that would yield better results, as well as means for ensuring that regulatory limits are adhered to—in other words, enforcement. To ensure fairness and effectiveness, those entrusted with establishing regulatory limits must be unbiased, un-captured by regulated interests, and also highly qualified. They must have the tools to develop and access the best, most comprehensive information, yet also have a broad degree of acceptance by the public they serve. Although this is extremely challenging, there are models to work from: judicial systems, "blue ribbon" panels, supreme audit institutions, and existing ecological management institutions, among many others. The Adirondack Park Agency in New York State already exhibits most of these attributes, and has been so effective in its difficult job that the "Adirondack Park Model" for habitat preservation has been adopted, with similar success, in many other parts of the world, including India and the coast of British Columbia.[34] The Global Reserve and Trusteeships should be endowed with these attributes and enlisted to support the regulatory role.

Decisions to regulate must be made rigorously, with humility and seriousness. The starting point must be the accumulated evidence and knowledge on the limits of the earth and its ecosystems to withstand the impacts of economic activity. As well, the approach must acknowledge that in many cases nothing short of regulatory limits shored up with an effective enforcement regime, with adequate compliance inspections and fines that deter violations, will produce the behavior changes needed to avoid ecological decline or collapse.

Regulatory authority should also be exercised in conjunction with the precautionary principle. The precautionary principle, remember, says that if the consequences of an action are unknown, but are judged to have some potential for major or irreversible negative consequences, then it is better to avoid that action, pending additional research. Precaution implies a strong measure of careful deliberation and highlights the need for high-quality, objective, and comprehensive information on the impacts of human action on the environment, broadly defined. Yet the principle has not been widely adopted because governments have not consistently applied it with a desired systemic end state in mind. Without a desired end state, governments applying the precautionary principle have trouble saying what we, their citizens, should be cautious *about*. The concept of right relationship and the integrity, resilience, and beauty of the commonwealth of life provides grounding for the precautionary principle.

The most difficult challenge in establishing a regulatory system will be extending it into areas where individual choice is considered sacrosanct in many societies. While many laws that limit individual freedom are readily accepted (for example, laws criminalizing murder or requiring one to stop at red lights), this authority will surely have to expand into new and challenging areas if human society is to work toward living within ecological limits. Laws regulating the number of children people can have, for example, would likely face serious resistance. Yet that kind of regulatory limit cannot responsibly be kept off the table if the only way to stay within the earth's ecological limits is to reduce population, and nonregulatory efforts or incentives are simply not working.

Consider a set of grandparents who have produced five humans two generations downstream: their grandchildren. Now compare them with another set that has produced over forty grandchildren. These different levels of procreation have significantly different costs for the earth's shared ecological heritage. Even if the set of forty grandchildren uses energy more efficiently in their lifetimes, the second set of grandparents has produced, two generations later, a greatly multiplied ecological—and carbon—footprint. If those grandchildren live in a developed country like Canada or the United States, the multiplier is even greater. If, on average, women of reproductive age had only one child, the human population would go back down to slightly more than 1 billion within only one hundred years[35]—a number equal to the population in 1804, and one that would be much more manageable for the biosphere.

The Role of the Global Federation in Setting Quotas for Member States

As the I=f(PATE) or similar framework is used to systematically analyze and define goals for reducing the human ecological impact, the rough shape of policy and practice options for a whole earth economy will come into view. Overall planetary goals, subject to frequent adjustment as new information becomes available and new technologies emerge, will have to be set. Nations within the Global Federation will have choices about the weight assigned to the four variables, so long as the total human impact (*I*) globally remains within their share of the earth's ecological limits. A nation that chooses to permit a large population may have to agree to a lower level of wealth, different technologies, or different practices, and conversely. An individual nation can use taxes or other environmental pricing mechanisms to create incentives for behavioral change with respect to the desired outcome. Tax incentives can be offered for certain technical innovations (*T*), for fewer children (*P*), for use of public transit and the like (*E*), and for public service jobs that pay less but provide fulfillment (*A*). There is nothing new, revolutionary, or threatening in these ideas. The Global Federation can do the same thing. It can tax individuals directly to alter one of the variables or a component thereof. Or, it can tax nations to ensure compliance, or offer grants to provide incentives. A wide portfolio of real possibilities can be imagined.

Taxing Authority of the Global Federation

Within the quotas set by the Global Reserve, human society will continue to use the earth and the life on it. Within those quotas, uses of the commons, such as the oceans, the air and atmosphere, fresh water, the products of photosynthesis, topsoil, thermal vents, and the like, should also be subject to taxes. The Trusteeships of Earth's Commons will be responsible for preventing confiscation and abuse of the commons by the wealthy and powerful, as has been the norm in much of history. In addition, the Global Federation should retain authority to tax these uses and, everything else being equal, to use the revenues to support those institutions that guide the running of the "earth household." Using the taxes for general revenues is likely preferable to having them earmarked for specific purposes no matter how worthy, as earmarking can create incentives to exploit rather than to conserve. The Alaska Permanent Fund, which distributes oil revenues to that state's citizens, for example, creates incentives for exploration and consumption rather than conservation. This in turn creates political pressure to maximize oil development. One way to help ensure the trustees' independence is not to let these incentives arise to begin with.

The Global Federation and the subsidiary governments should impose severance taxes on extractions from the earth's crust (the lithosphere), such as oil, coal, gas, mineral, and metal deposits. Some extractions should be discouraged or eliminated. For example, gold mining is often extremely damaging to the biosphere and often to miners themselves, yet is hardly essential because most of it is used for jewelry or for sale as hedges against currency instability. Limiting the use of gold for jewelry to gold already extracted is a small sacrifice that would benefit life's commonwealth. The main attraction of gold as a hedge is its scarcity value—a commodity that cannot easily be created. Its use for this purpose can be rendered unnecessary by the creation of an artificial scarcity, such as in ecors, or in limited coins or artifacts. The Global Federation could wield its taxing authority to work toward eliminating or finding substitutes for metal compounds that are persistent and harmful in the biosphere.

Global taxation is also warranted on income of individuals and corporations, with the goal of reducing or eliminating tax havens—jurisdictions that levy little or no tax and serve only for wealth building. An international alternative minimum tax should be established so that no one can escape paying a fair share to support the global commonwealth of life.

A Global Court

The principal purpose of the Global Court is to prevent the abuse of power of global agencies, or their subsidiaries, and to hear cases of enforcement of global rules.

A whole earth economy should be based on the informed, scientifically based rule of law. The "rule of law" means that global regulatory limits required to meet ecological limits and ensure fair sharing of the earth's bounty must be respected. Resistance to these limits because of ideals of national sovereignty and the desire of certain countries to dominate the economy needs to fall away. In a successful system of governance, regulation can play a determinative role—as has happened, by and large, with environmental laws in the United States, incomplete though they are. And while existing international judicial bodies tasked with enforcing this global justice are weak, they are in a process of evolution that serves as a useful template for the future.

The World Court (also called the International Court of Justice, or ICJ) located in The Hague, Netherlands, was established in 1946 under the auspices of the United Nations to replace the Permanent Court of International Justice, which functioned under the League of Nations. In 2002 the International Criminal Court (ICC) was formed as a permanent body to hear cases involving crimes against humanity, war crimes, and genocide.

Two revisions to these courts are needed. First, the international community should expand the courts' powers to recognize as prosecutable those civil and criminal offenses that are "harmful to natural systems," such as illegal actions that threaten species with extinction, or excessive emissions of gases that contribute to global warming. The existing ICC could offer a better venue for these issues at present, as long as its jurisdiction were expanded. In the World

Court, jurisdiction over a case occurs only if the nations involved agree to its being heard, and nongovernmental organizations and individuals have no standing, either as plaintiffs or as friends of the court. The World Court also lacks robust enforcement mechanisms. While the UN Charter requires that all states abide by this court's findings, cases where nations do not comply are merely referred to the Security Council where its members (the United States, China, Britain, France, and Russia) can exercise their veto. Accordingly, it is ineffective in controlling some of the worst of the current economic rogue states.

The ICC has jurisdiction strictly over nations that are members. Since China, India, and the United States currently do not plan to become members, this is a significant shortcoming in the operation of the court. Yet, as global government is established to preserve and enhance the commonwealth of life, the ICC or something like it could evolve into the court of reference for global governance: a Global Court. All nations that make up the Federation would be subordinate to it for matters set forth in a Global Federal constitution, just as Europe has developed enforceable rules that limit individual nations' sovereignty in numerous areas. The Global Court would also have jurisdiction over disputes concerning Trusteeships of Earth's Commons—such as the nature and issuance of extraction and "tipping" permits, the sharing of profits, and so on. It would also review the operations of the Global Reserve and treaties between or among member nations in areas relevant to global jurisdiction. Compliance with the court's decisions could be enforced by denying nations the rights to use the universal currency or the right to trade. Rogue states could be punished by losing their citizens' shares from the global trust fund and by other measures similar to today's economic sanctions used to encourage international cooperation. To have a chance of working in a timely manner, the Global Court would need to have a hierarchy with a presence at various levels, such as regional and national. At the same time, national and subnational jurisdictions would retain the right to embody independent judicial systems to govern matters where global rules would not be applicable, such as education, public safety, culture, and so forth. As in provincial and state courts under current federal systems, this would allow the emergence of jurisprudence specific to less-than-global circumstances.

Toward Global Governance for All of Life's Commonwealth

The current de facto system of global governance, with its laissez-faire underpinnings, is following a trajectory that provides much more to fear than new and more rigorous global governance functions or institutions with effective regulatory authority, which at the same time provide the minimum level of jurisdiction and authority needed to ensure an economy in right relationship with life's commonwealth. Considerable capability already exists in the world for monitoring and projecting trends and for identifying causal relationships with regard to global warming, loss of biodiversity, chronic air and water pollution, and other elements of the current crisis. The need is to integrate these separate capabilities and to give them a new focus: reining in economic development so that it no longer pushes past the ecological limits of the earth.

A Global Reserve, Trusteeships for Global Commons, a Global Federation, and a Global Court provide ways to envision an effective system for fulfilling the functions now missing at the global level. If other governance options would better achieve the same objectives, not only are they welcome—they are urgently needed.

Conclusion

Four Steps to a Whole Earth Economy

A crisis is a terrible thing to waste. It makes unthinkable changes suddenly possible.

—Book review of Melvyn Leffler's *For the Soul of Mankind: The United States, the Soviet Union, and the Cold War*

IN 1968, ANTHROPOLOGIST GREGORY BATESON organized a week-long conference in Austria on the Effects of Conscious Purpose on Human Adaptation, under the auspices of the Wenner-Gren Foundation for Anthropological Research. He assembled world leaders in the science and humanities, such as biologist Barry Commoner, to spend this time in reflection and dialogue. He asked them to consider the question "whether human consciousness perhaps especially as it is shaped in modern western culture, 'might contain systematic distortions of view which, when implemented by modern technology, become destructive of the balances between individual man, human society, and the ecosystem of the planet.'"[1]

In other words, can conscious purpose affect the course of human adaptation—or, more darkly, is consciousness, especially that of Western culture, tragically, perhaps fatally, distorted? The significance of the conference lay in the fact that this question would even be asked at the time, and that some of the world's top thinkers would spend a week struggling with it. Forty years ago, the crisis of a mismatch between natural processes and human mental capacities was already looming large on the horizon of the earth's future.

Today the question is far more urgent. The irrational pursuit of economic growth despite growing ecological strain is a clear sign of a distorted consciousness, yet right relationship offers the hope for a more optimistic prognosis than a "fatal" one. The human prospect is fully immersed in an ecological crisis, and our options are narrowing into a range of high-risk scenarios. In simplified terms, this collective crisis presents the people of the world and their decision makers with two choices. The first choice is to allow the ecological crisis to develop until it becomes so obvious that the world's citizens and their leaders will be compelled to react. The second is to act now on the mounting evidence of coming catastrophes, by planning and implementing our way to a whole earth economy. How can we work to increase the chance that the second option is the one we choose?

The people of the world can bring about a right relationship between the human economy and the earth's commonwealth of life if we come together and take four steps:

- *Grounding and clarification:* All societies around the world need to develop a sense of awe for the cosmos and the earth, as well as an ethic based on deep respect for the integrity, resilience, and beauty of life's commonwealth. The principle of right relationship is a basis for this grounding and clarification.

- *Design:* Societies also must make it an urgent priority to develop institutional changes and processes necessary to enhance and preserve the integrity, resilience, and beauty of the commonwealth of life, with the benefit of history but thoroughly and thoughtfully adapted to the present. Models, pilot schemes, and broad-based plans must be rapidly developed so they will be ready to implement as the demand for change intensifies.

- *Witness:* Everyone who wants a future for an earth that supports life's commonwealth needs to commit to individual and collective changes that will lead to right relationship.

- *Nonviolent reform:* Quaker history contains many examples of nonviolent reform leading to right relationship, but the template for abolishing slavery is the most well known. This model and others can serve as the basis for building a whole earth economy in right relationship with life's commonwealth.

To imagine how all the people on the earth might possibly come together to take these steps, consider the usual way a new computer system is introduced into an organization. The new system is developed alongside the old one until the new system is advanced and bug-free enough to be brought in to replace the old. In the same way, work should start now to conceptualize, design, and set up new or reformed global institutions that can enhance the global common good so the world community can bring them into operation when opportunity arises.

This cannot be a plan only for experts and policy makers. People from all levels of society must be involved. Grounding and clarification about the need to cherish and protect the commonwealth will take hold through experiencing nature and after earnest conversations among people who care for each other, and not merely discussions in environmental or governance think tanks. Designing a rational new approach to economics will only work if people with diverse life experiences participate in dialogue about what they aspire to in their daily lives in a whole earth economy. People must bear witness, when working, playing, transacting, and relating to each other every day, so that these discussions will turn from *talk* into the *walk* of right relationship. To work, nonviolent reform must be a vast project of the world citizenry.

Social change of the magnitude that is now required has sometimes been evolutionary and sometimes triggered by great upheavals such as wars or economic depressions. Unfortunately, history also offers horrendous examples where change did not happen in time. Scenarios that predict massive social disorder and ecological ruin because of the way the world economy is run have gained enough credence already to begin to galvanize a movement for global environmental governance for the common good. But there is not much time left to do so.

Grounding and Clarification: A Spiritual Basis for Action

Deep apprehension about the convergence of ecological, economic, and social crises is widespread. Global recognition of these crises is reflected in the commitment to sustainable development made in the 1972 Stockholm and the 1992 Rio declarations, as well as in the 2000 Earth Charter (more on that later), as yet words awaiting meaningful action. Many cultural analysts, social thinkers, and religious leaders see a profound spiritual crisis at the heart of this situation. This crisis is about human identity within the unfurling creativity of the cosmos and how it plays out on the earth.

The solution to this crisis is grounded in right relationship and a deep respect for the integrity, resilience, and beauty of human and natural communities. Essential to this is a shift from an egocentric—"I," "me," "mine"—values perspective, to one of collaborative engagement in pursuit of the common good. The combined moral power of the human community must provide the baseline orientation for the changes in global governance that were proposed in Chapter 5. Grounding and clarification on what all people should see as a common purpose has already begun, with what Paul Hawken calls "the greatest movement in the world."[2] Even those who think that humans are all that matters from a moral point of view and see no reason to be passionate about the well-being of the rest of the commonwealth of life should care about their own children's and grandchildren's ecological and economic survival. Human societies are embedded in the environment and depend on it. Surely, we can all pull together—if only for the benefit of our own future generations.

Design: An Informed Plan for the Future

As Gregory Bateson suggests, with some significant exceptions, Western civilization has not managed to clearly present the factors that have led to the ecological overshoot of modern civilization in a way that sheds light on how humanity can survive the current environmental crisis. Hence, the design phase that will lead the planet toward a whole earth economy requires a broad review of human historical experience, along with sober reflection on the best scientific information on life's prospect under various scenarios. These steps will help us find ways to develop institutional arrangements that will drive the economy toward right relationship.

Lessons from History and Modeling the Future

Over the past several decades, researchers from a number of fields have started piecing together a new kind of history—the history of the global ecosystem and of human adaptation to the earth's environments.[3] Environmental history makes it possible to develop models of trends and map out scenarios of future changes. As ecosystem historians and modelers have gathered information, their models and scenarios have become increasingly credible. Nonetheless, working from the earth's history to envision the future has limitations, and in fact a disturbing trend is becoming apparent: Future forecasts have often turned out to be far too rosy.

Several significant environmental changes foreseen through modeling and scenario building are happening much faster than expected. For example, in 2001, the International Panel on Climate Change (IPCC) predicted significant melting of the Arctic ice cap by 2100, but by 2007 scientists were predicting that greenhouses gases now present in the atmosphere will decrease the polar ice cap by some 40 percent by the year 2050, and already that estimate seems too optimistic.[4]

The evolutionary biologist and bio-geographer Jared Diamond has helped to pioneer a method of analyzing how past civilizations did or did not avert ecological catastrophe.[5] His work is useful for trying to avoid future failures and drawing hope from the successes. He identifies four categories of failure: (1) failure to anticipate, (2) failure to recognize, (3) failure to attempt to solve, and (4) attempts that failed.

Failure to anticipate deals with cases where societies deliberately changed the environment, with unforeseen harmful effects. For example, Australian settlers who introduced foxes and rabbits into Australia in the 1800s did not appreciate the damage they eventually would do to the native ecology.[6]

Failure to recognize occurs when societies do not realize that they have caused adverse effects. Examples are soil degradation in Australia, in southeast Polynesia, and in most of the western United States. Failure of this kind includes changes that were not readily visible and that happened gradually.

An example of the failure to attempt to solve known or anticipated problems is acid mine drainage from mining operations in Montana, especially before 1971 when there was no law requiring companies to clean up mining sites. This category contains instances of powerful elites that charged ahead despite the harm they were causing to the common good. Canada's rampant and globally irresponsible development of its oil-rich tar sands is a tragic contemporary example.

Failed attempts to address problems are what happens when, for example, perverse subsidies in fisheries and agriculture both hasten and intensify ecological collapse, which ends up hurting the fishers and farmers the subsidies were supposed to benefit.

Diamond also describes leaders and societies that have avoided ecological catastrophes. The Tokugawa shoguns in the 1600s recognized that Japan's timber consumption was increasing through the building of houses and ships and the use of wood fuel for cooking and industry. In that case, the shoguns met the challenge of deforestation by controlling supply and demand. When Joaquín Balaguer came to office for the second time as president of the Dominican Republic in 1966, he recognized the need for maintaining forested watersheds for energy and water requirements. He took drastic action against rich and powerful families, and even used the army to close down illegal logging and expel squatters. In 1994, for example, the army drove bulldozers through luxury houses built within Juan B. Pérez National Park.

More recently, the Chinese instituted mandatory population control measures that decreased the rate of growth to 1.3 percent per year by 2001, though the ultimate success of this controversial measure is still not known.[7] These examples may provide some hope as we turn to solutions to the momentous ecological crises we now face.

The Dahlem Konferenzen, or Dahlem Workshops, have included admirable attempts to promote the science that will be needed for such solutions. Initiated in Berlin in 1974 in response to increasing specialization in science, the Dahlem Workshops are designed to promote the interdisciplinary exchange of ideas among scientists. Each workshop is a multidisciplinary conference that brings together about 40 leading researchers in life, earth, social, and cultural sciences to promote joint scientific inquiry in areas of international interest bedeviled by significant knowledge gaps.[8] Two recent Dahlem Workshop reports, *Earth System Analysis for Sustainability* (2003) and *Sustainability or Collapse? An Integrated History and Future of People on Earth* (2005),[9] show how history can be used to develop global templates for reaching desirable outcomes and avoiding undesirable ones. These workshops integrate earth-science research, social and economic analysis, studies of mental and cultural development, and geographic and ecosystem studies to give a better understanding of how the human economy can improve the human prospect—or worsen it.

These two Dahlem Workshop reports provide high-quality, science-based scenarios that describe likely futures for the human–earth relationship, depending on the economic choices that human society makes. They provide a vast amount of accurate information on future trends, even if a measure of uncertainty remains. However, should the dangers emerge in ways different than anticipated (and often they are worse and also more complex than anticipated), it will still have been better to act on the information available than to continue with a business-as-usual scenario that has an even higher likelihood of leading to catastrophe.

Jared Diamond and others have provided plenty of evidence of what can happen if such information is ignored or cynically downplayed. The Dahlem Workshops, multiplied many times over, are precisely the kind of effort we need to design our way out of our ecological predicament.

Institutional Change: Reacting to Crisis or Managing Evolution

If there is still time to choose between reacting to and averting the worst of the ecological crisis that has already begun, it is running short. When decision makers are in a crisis, they look for alternative models and systems that work. The preferred path is one of taking seriously the mounting evidence of the impending ecological crisis and, before it is too late, designing and implementing the institutional responses necessary to address them. The more that can be done now to design and test models of governance that respond to the global environmental crisis, the more alternatives will be "on the shelf" to guide decisions on how to build a whole earth economy.

Societies have usually undergone whole-scale institutional change gradually, over considerable time, or in periods of major social and political disorder. The European Union, for example, begun in 1952 with the European Coal and Steel Community, has, over the past fifty years, evolved into a powerful, yet adaptive, constitutional structure that integrates the European economy while establishing some mandatory EU-wide environmental and social safety-net norms. International institutions such as the United Nations, the World Bank, the World Trade Organization, and the International Labor Organization continue to suffer from political domination by growth-oriented corporations and governments and have strong internal cultures that are resistant to change.

True, these international organizations do have agendas and some well-developed programs and expertise for safeguarding the global common good and, in theory, they talk about addressing the long-term consequences of economic growth. In practice, however, their ecological and social goals take a back seat to business interests' free trade and investment pressures. The hope that current international institutions can evolve in appropriate, timely ways with regard to global environmental governance is therefore highly tenuous. The current ecological crisis requires urgent action.

The hope that current international institutions can evolve in appropriate, timely ways with regard to global environmental governance is highly tenuous.

Yet climate change, overpopulation, deforestation, resource depletion, and other growing ecological threats present an opportunity, as well as a challenge. Many of these issues have languished on the international agenda for decades, but the climate crisis is bringing new and sustained attention to them. Decision makers and opinion leaders may well be tempted to focus on issues like climate change with a leisurely, business-as-usual approach, but the growing urgency of the ecological threats to human society will make that response less and less acceptable to the world's citizens. More and more people are realizing that if the crisis runs unchecked, it will likely end what we think of as "modern civilization."[10] When the world is in crisis and conflict, opportunities arise to fundamentally alter political and economic systems.

The Earth Charter is an example of civil society's growing impatience with the global political impasse that blocks progress on the as-yet-toothless commitments that the international community has made to maintaining global ecological integrity over a long period. Originally a project of the World Commission on Environment and Development (the Brundtland Commission), in 1994 the Earth Charter became a civil society initiative after a draft UN Earth Charter failed to be adopted at the 1992 Rio Earth Summit. The initiative used a consultative process, engaging civil society and academia, and the drafting process drew in more than five thousand comments worldwide. After its formal launch in The Hague, Netherlands, in 2000, the Earth Charter Initiative began an endorsement campaign, through which the Charter has gained the endorsement of some twenty-five hundred organizations and over four hundred towns and cities. As of 2007, the governments of Brazil and Mexico, along with subnational jurisdictions in Australia, Canada, Germany, and elsewhere, made public commitments to promote Earth Charter principles in their domestic and international affairs.[11]

Another global effort that holds strong potential to assist in the transition to a whole earth economy is the International Union of Conservation and Nature (IUCN).[12] Established in 1948, the IUCN is a global environmental network with over one thousand government and nongovernment member organizations and more than ten times that number of scientists and environmental professional members, with a presence in some 160 countries. The IUCN mission is "to influence, encourage and assist societies throughout the world to conserve the integrity and diversity of nature and to ensure that any use of natural resources is equitable and ecologically sustainable."[13] Engaging existing platforms like the IUCN for merging scientific research with policy dialogue will be essential in building a whole earth economy.

Designing New or Reformed Global Institutions

If current international institutions are not likely to respond to the current ecological crisis without significant reform, is there a way to trigger a shift to effective global environmental governance within the ten-year span that many scientists say we have to take action to prevent global warming's worst catastrophes?[14] Is it possible to use available or emerging models and suggestions, such as those in the preceding chapter, to develop a critical path? While the movement in the eighteenth century to end the political economy of slavery in Great Britain was successful within a fairly short time, it had the advantage of being a single-issue campaign. In addition, the British Parliament had the power to enforce its decisions on slavery, and because Britain was the sea power of the day, it had the capacity to enforce the decision at the international level.

The critical changes needed today are far more multidimensional and complex. They involve the establishment of appropriate global decision-making functions before some of the necessary changes can be introduced. Chapter 5 described the kind of global governance that will be needed to provide equitable stewardship governance for the global commons. These proposals are visionary, far reaching, and complex. As with all complex arrangements, the process will require organizing the tasks involved into manageable parts and logical sequences. The following are some of the questions relevant to the establishment of a critical path for establishing new forms of global governance that will be needed in a whole earth economy.

- Has the concept or institution been developed enough that its implementation can be readily comprehended, and has it been provided with sufficient support to become operational?
- Are there pilot schemes or working examples in parts of the world that can be used to show how the application or institution can work and be used?
- Can the concept or institution be developed in one or more countries or regions, so that it can run alongside existing systems until the new system is working well enough to phase out the old one?
- Since some of these proposals will take longer to become operational than others, can they be started earlier?
- Is it possible to identify a critical path for reaching the goals envisioned?

The Global Court   A Global Court is relatively easy to envision. As already discussed, the basic template of the existing International Court of Justice and the International Criminal Court could be adapted to this expanded use. To some extent, a Global Court will depend on the other proposals, but the first three criteria above pose no serious problems to its setup and functioning.

The Global Reserve   While in theory the federal monetary reserves of many nations provide a starting point, the Global Reserve described in the previous chapter needs more conceptual development. At the moment it lacks pilot schemes or working examples, and it does not have systems running in parallel to existing systems. The UN Environment Programme and other United Nations agencies, the Global Environmental Fund, the IPCC, the World Bank, and other international financial institutions already have much of the expertise and capability to perform functions that would be housed in a Global Reserve or other similar institution. But, as noted in the previous chapter, proposals to reform global institutions intended to protect the environment have failed to tackle the economics of unlimited growth.

So, how could a Global Reserve be developed? Work of the kind that the Global Reserve would have to undertake is already being done, as a few examples show. Previous chapters described the I=f(PATE) framework and how it can provide the basis for the work of a Global Reserve, and many researchers have analyzed how variations of the framework could assist policy development.[15] The ecological footprint developed by William Rees and Mathis Wackernagel in 1996 is widely regarded as one of the best available comprehensive indicators of environmental impact, though it is not without its difficulties.[16] The science of global ecosystem assessment is producing an evolving picture of the human impact in terms of net primary productivity, ecosystem biomass, biodiversity, and other key variables.[17]

Also relevant in considering the work of the Global Reserve are case studies of regions and communities that have attained a high level of well-being with a relatively low level of ecological impact. An example is the state of Kerala, India. Although its average income is sixty times less than in the United States, with per capita consumption and ecological footprints typical of the developing world, its quality of life indicators based on education, health care, fertility rates, and the like nevertheless rank quite high on the world scale.[18] Kerala's success has been attributed to a communal spirit of cooperation, a sense of the earth's efficiency, reliance on local production, the high status of women, a strong sense of grassroots democracy, and a social agenda aimed at providing for society's weakest members.[19] Amish communities in the United States, too, are a noteworthy if imperfect example. They have a long tradition of introducing new technologies only after the community's careful consideration of whether they are truly needed.

Design of the Global Reserve should begin with comprehensive reviews of these and other analytic techniques, assessments, and case studies, to determine how they can be brought together. Part of this initial process is to examine the many capacities and functions related to this work that already exist in UNEP and other international organizations. It makes sense to see whether and how that work can be integrated and put into a logical framework that fulfills the functions for which the Global Reserve is proposed. The categories of allocation, scale, and distribution must be more fully elaborated to establish a global ecological budget in which allowable impact on the biosphere, not money, is the underlying analytical foundation. Additional conceptual work is also needed with respect to the development of transitional budgets and implementation plans based on the global budgets. This conceptual work needs to be placed at the front of determining the critical path to fulfilling the proposed functions of the Global Reserve.

Global Trusteeships The Trusteeship concept described in the previous chapter fully meets the first criterion of being readily comprehended. The basic purpose of the trusts is to ensure the ecological integrity of global common property resources, while providing a fair allocation and distribution of benefits and burdens among humans and between humans and other species. As with the Global Reserve concept, the capability and expertise to conduct analytical work needed for the trusts' functions already exists in various organizations, and tapping into what already exists is an important initial step.

The Trusteeship concept, at present, has no closely relevant working examples at the global level, though the Alaska Permanent Fund that holds a portion of oil revenues in trust for the state's citizens has many comparable features, as do numerous land trusts around the world. Scores of indigenous reserves and communities around the globe also have set up trust-based management systems that are relevant. One example is the Yakama Nation in eastern Washington State, which manages a 12-million-acre timber and farming resource and distributes the revenues equally. It fully supports all members of its community, while consciously maintaining the beauty, resilience, and integrity of the land for the future.

Will it be possible to achieve coordinated governance of the global commons by persuading all national governments to agree to such trusts? Is it possible, for example, to divide the atmosphere and its use into 192 allocations corresponding to the number of countries in the world?[20] Dysfunctional, criminal, and failed states, or states with strong views on proprietary use of a commons resource, may well prevent the trust approach from successfully protecting the commons, just as countries like Norway, Iceland, and especially Japan have found absurd rationales to justify whale hunting, despite decades of international bans.

The experience of Arvid Pardo, a Maltese diplomat, is instructive in this regard. He became the "father" of the Law of the Sea Conference because of the electrifying speech he made in 1967 before the UN General Assembly. He called for international regulations to ensure peace at sea, to prevent further pollution of the oceans, and to protect the entire marine resource. He proposed that the seabed constitutes part of the "common heritage of mankind," a phrase that appears in Article 136 of the UN Convention on the Law of the Sea, and asked that some of the sea's wealth be used to bankroll a fund that would help close the gap between rich and poor nations. He urged the United Nations to create a new kind of international agency, as a trustee for all countries, that would assume jurisdiction over the seabed and supervise how its resources are exploited. He called for the net financial benefits, which he hoped would be considerable, to be used primarily to promote the development of poor countries.

Despite the long and tireless work of many global-minded people for a Law of the Sea that would work in this way, the final document reserved "Exclusive Economic Zones" for the proprietary interests of national governments. Pardo lamented that the common heritage of mankind had been whittled down to a few fish and a little seaweed. According to Richard Falk, the private sector engineered this result with heavy lobbying, much aided by the neoliberal politics of the United States and Britain.[21] A better route for the implementation of Trusteeships at a global level remains to be developed. It is not clear that Trusteeships for global commons can be brought into being independently of a global parliament. If this is the case, the early development of such a parliament is critical.

The Global Federation   The concept of global federalism meets the first two criteria of having existing templates and operational support. People already know what a parliament is, as examples abound at a national level. The European Union is relevant in this case, though a bit more complicated. The EU lies somewhere between an international organization and a state.[22] It consists largely of a set of intergovernmental and supranational institutions supported by a pact among elites, without deep loyalty, a common identity, or mutual support. In mapping out approaches to this kind of federal structure and process, there is much to be said for keeping the chosen model simple.[23] As the European Union expands, that model is gradually being tested.

Even though global federalism is at least imaginable, it raises many weighty questions. How is the principle of subsidiarity to be understood and practiced within the context of global federalism? What areas of decision making and control are most appropriate, and at what levels of government? How can transparency and accountability be ensured? How can federalism avoid bureaucratic corruption, dominance by larger national countries, and capture by transnational companies and the wealthy elite? How many elected members should there be, and what method should be used to elect them? What will be the rules for decision making? What will happen in nondemocratic countries? How will minorities be protected?

The experience of the European Union will provide some guidance, yet there is considerable (though not insurmountable) work to be done in making operational the concepts of global federalism. The case of Norway, in relation to the EU, offers an example of the complexities involved. The people of that nation, in a referendum, declined to join the EU because doing so would have required them to lower their standards on social benefits, economic equity, labor rights, and environmental protection. The new global federalism will have to avoid the trap of sinking down to the lowest common denominator, which is the tendency when institutions are expanded to include many members.

If a Global Federation is to be established, the highly unequal sizes of the existing 192 countries require that the basis of global participation be rethought. The unifying idea is the common need of the entire global community to have clear rules on how our global commons is used and shared, and how the global community can share the earth's limited capacity to use the power of the sun to cyclically renew life. Because the United Nations is the current forum for bringing the nations of the world together on global issues and has expertise and capabilities in many of the areas for which governance reform is needed, reform of the UN and its agencies so as to ensure that this unifying idea takes hold is a possibility to examine and consider. Doing so would entail integrating the relevant functions of existing UN and other international agencies under common direction and oversight. Most important of all, effective reform would have to come from a new orientation of right

Effective reform must come from a new orientation of right relationship that gives respect for life on earth higher priority than short-term profit and continuous growth.

relationship that gives respect for life on earth higher priority than short-term profit and continuous growth.

In addition to these questions on the nature of global federalism, the matter of independent funding must be considered. UN Secretary-General Kofi Annan once observed that *"the United Nations is the only fire brigade that must go out and buy a fire engine before it can respond to an emergency."*[24] Countries like the United States condition their massive funding of the UN on the adoption of policies or practices they support, which illustrates that the issue of institutional financing is less about money and more about political control.[25] For example, local government in Japan has a weak financial base. It is heavily supported and therefore controlled by the central government. If the Global Federation is to be properly equipped to carry out its mission, it will need taxing authority.

Based on this discussion, a summary of a critical path for developing the global institutions needed for a whole earth economy is described in the following table.

Critical Paths for Four Proposed Global Institutions

Proposed Institution	Is the concept ready for implementation?	Do pilot programs or examples exist?	Are regional or national pilots possible?	What time frame is required?
Global Reserve	No	No	Yes	Long
Trusts for Commons	Yes, with adaptations to global level	Yes, at sub-national level	Yes	Medium
Global Federation	Yes, with adaptations to global level	Yes, with adaptations to global level	Yes	Long
Global Court	Yes	Yes, but modification to global level needed	Numerous examples exist	Short

Witness: Toward a Mass Epiphany

As we make the personal choices we must make each day, we face the dilemma of being dependent on a society that causes ecological destruction we abhor. We cannot turn away from the modern world, yet we must curb our demands so that the earth's resources are sustained. We are called to show, by our daily choices and actions, the way toward a more harmonious, more fulfilling, nondestructive way for humans to live on our planet—the way to harvest the fruit without destroying the tree. We are called to celebrate the beauty, diversity, and complexity of life, and to engage in the difficult but ultimately joyful work of practicing right relationship within the whole commonwealth of life.

But how will the collective action of individuals come together? From where will come guidance on the kind of action needed to build a whole earth economy? The complex interplay between governments, commerce, and civil society, compounded by the limitations of international governance institutions, restricts initiative and hampers rapid decision making. Yet these are the arenas where change ultimately must occur. The initiatives needed are likely to come with the emergence in any or all of these sectors of new champions and leaders willing to break from the binds of conventional thinking and able to inspire a mass epiphany underlying a broad call for a new way.

Within the complicated web of international, national, and local links, and among government, commercial, and civil society sectors, it is impossible to predict just how change will happen. The inspired leadership built on a strong ethic of right relationship, which is necessary to trigger a kind of mass witness to the need for transforming the human–earth relationship, could emerge from government, from business, or even from civil society.

There are change agents as well as status quo supporters in all three sectors. Each category offers examples of success *and* failure. Wealthy people sometimes do admirable things with their money;

some companies are progressive and visionary; some governments have adopted effective programs. In all these sectors, care and concern for the future of human and other life on the planet in the face of climate change and other ecological threats is a growing topic of discussion. Civil society in particular has begun to show unity on global warming and in efforts like the Earth Charter.

The change will come when a convincing case is made, built on honest information about what is needed for right relationship between human beings and the earth, and what our lives will be like in a whole earth economy. And more and more, the case is being made. For example, in his book *Managing Without Growth*,[26] Peter Victor shows how Canada could retain its high quality of life, reduce poverty, and improve its respect for the earth's limits in the context of steady-state economics.

Leadership from those in public office is more likely to follow changes in public opinion, rather than begin them. As Henry David Thoreau said: "statesmen and legislators, standing so completely within the institution, never distinctly and nakedly behold it. They speak of moving society, but have no resting place without it."[27] This means that each individual citizen has the biggest role of all in the coming change, whether as a consumer, a voter, or a member. Bearing witness is a matter of moving from conviction to action in a way that strikes a chord of common sense, rings loud and clear, and soon has others joining in the joyful music. Public opinion is the collective wisdom of human society, and history proves that almost any kind of governance, however odd or revolutionary, can control society *if* it enjoys the support of the majority of its citizenry.

Nonviolent Reform: Working to Build a Whole Earth Economy

History is replete with stories of violent change that destroyed and devastated the material world and shook the human spirit. Violent change is a wrong relationship between humans and each other and between humans and the rest of the world. The path of right relationship must be built on nonviolent reform. One prominent historical example of how nonviolent action led to dramatic change is the campaign over many generations to end legal slavery.[28] As noted in the Preface to this book, a group composed mostly of Quakers founded the Society for Effecting the Abolition of Slavery in England in 1787. They recruited Thomas Clarkson to lead them in an organized campaign to ban slavery within the British Empire. As a Cambridge debater, Clarkson was already well versed on the issue. He turned his speeches into a manuscript, which was published by a Quaker bookshop; the work was widely read, and Clarkson became the leading public figure for the network of Quakers and their allies as they began to build the antislavery movement. William Wilberforce, a non-Quaker, became the person associated with abolition because he brought the successful antislavery bill through the British Parliament in 1807. At the time, nonconformists to the Church of England could not serve in Parliament, so Quakers could not be directly involved in legislative action.

The process the movement adopted was to gather evidence and present it to a British public largely apathetic about the slavery issue. The Society distributed striking posters depicting the diagram of the ship *Brookes*, showing how slaves were inhumanely shipped like cargo. They distributed pamphlets and organized many hundreds of public meetings, and they also led a boycott of slave-grown sugar. In 1791, a rebellion of slaves on Saint-Domingue led to the establishment of Haiti, the world's only country composed of freed slaves. The Society's action made the cost of enforcing slavery enormously higher, a practical factor in the adoption of Wilberforce's bill. The British government compensated former slave owners.

Many subsequent reformers, such as those who sought to end the death penalty in Great Britain and the United States, used the antislavery campaign as a model.[29] Exposing the facts of the slave trade to public awareness was key to a dramatic turnaround in the public's moral assessment of the issue. According to *The Economist*, it was the shame and degradation that the slave trade and the slave economy brought to those involved, perpetrators as well as victims, that proved its undoing,[30] even as the shame of wearing the skins of endangered animals today has largely ended that practice in public.

The poster of the slave ship *Brookes*, graphically displaying the way Africans were being transported, was a prime catalyst in creating the political climate that led to slavery's banning. Many decades later, footage of a whale being harpooned by Russians helped turn the fledgling organization Greenpeace into an international force. The 2006 film *An Inconvenient Truth* has played a similar role in the campaign on climate change. A serious grassroots campaign can undoubtedly uncover other images, even in this time of jaded sensibilities, that can lift awareness of the need for true environmental governance.

This is the kind of public outreach and alternative policy work that needs to be done on the global environmental crisis. All people and all communities who understand the crisis of the human–earth relationship need to act urgently. Although humankind is made up of many different cultures and values, the global environmental crisis unites us all. Everyone concerned about the future of spaceship earth needs to join together in a sustained commitment to change the global economic and governance order. The question is straightforward: Will future generations of humans and the rest of life's commonwealth have hope for life on this planet?

The antislavery model contains a variety of action-oriented steps useful for any movement focused on global, nonviolent reform. They include: evidence gathering, a publicity campaign, boycotting, legislative reform, and outright nonviolent rebellion. Likewise, building a whole earth economy and the global institutions needed to support it can proceed in the following way.

> *Will future generations of humans and the rest of life's commonwealth have hope for life on this planet?*

1. *Gather evidence and prepare case studies, pilot projects, and plans.* Just as informing the British public helped build a mass movement to end slavery, the world's citizens today need evidence that helps make the case for a whole earth economy. Many groups and institutions have already spent decades systematically gathering an enormous amount of this kind of evidence. The extensive reports of the IPCC on global warming that came out in 2007 and on previous occasions,[31] UNEP's Global Environment Outlook (GEO) series of reports on the world environment,[32] the annual State of the World report of the Worldwatch Institute,[33] the Dahlem Workshop reports, the World Wildlife Fund's Living Planet Report on the global ecological footprint,[34] as well as George Monbiot's searching analysis in his book *Heat* of current technologies that attempt to address global warming—all provide a mere sampling of what is available. The UN agencies, international financial institutions, and other international organizations have entire programs devoted to generating evidence and analysis that can help build a whole earth economy. Because some of this evidence is of higher quality than others, and some is presented in a context that assumes that indiscriminate economic growth must rise no matter what, honest assessment of the available information is essential.

   The current challenge is to consolidate the highest quality evidence on the ecological threats that arise from our current economy and to present the consequences of endless growth to the public with complete honesty. With this now virtually irrefutable evidence in hand, along with the tools to continually update it, an appropriate organization or partnership of organizations can prepare case studies, pilot schemes, and broad plans for how a whole earth economy would work and how new global governance functions should be developed and organized. This work will require people capable of understanding and then conceptualizing the relationships between the earth and the human economy. A broadly inclusive organization like the IUCN could certainly play a most helpful role, and it is essential that participants include representatives of the UN agencies and other international organizations already working to understand these relationships. The Dahlem Workshops provide one excellent model for bringing together multidisciplinary researchers and specialists. Other workshops can be organized to map out solutions to global-scale problems, with an allocation of tasks among teams. The Pugwash Conferences[35] that lay the groundwork for a moral response by scientists on global peace, and the annual conferences of the Global Ecological Integrity Group[36] are other examples.

Platforms or models like these are well-suited to assembling working teams to draft methodologies for test cases and pilot projects and to seek out countries and subnational regions that might participate in governance pilot projects and models. From analysis of case studies and pilot projects, plans for global institutions such as the Trusteeships, Global Federation, Global Reserve, and Global Court suggested in this book can be developed, taking into account how they will work together. The principles set out in the Earth Charter, which resulted from a broad, participatory global process over several years, provide an exemplary foundation for harnessing high-quality, honest scientific research to governance structures.

The work at this stage must be undertaken with the recognition that any plans that develop will require ongoing evolution as public outreach is undertaken; wise leaders will seek to engage the public, not dictate to it, to gather support. Although many scholars and researchers are giving thought to global environmental issues, their ideas need to expand out from academic and professional audiences and move into more popular, multidisciplinary forums. Full consideration must also be given to the intercultural factors involved in making a global governance strategy democratically viable in various spheres worldwide. Cultures that are usually marginalized—traditional and native groups, or isolated minorities like the Bedouin in Israel, or the many culturally splintered groups of the Balkans or of western China—must be sought out to become active participants, particularly when it comes to thinking through plans for a global parliament and Global Trusteeships.

2. *Publicize, educate, and involve.* The next stage is to promulgate the case for a whole earth economy, including the need for major reform of global governance through developing new or reformed global institutions. Because the global community must eventually come on board, this outreach needs to use as many forms of communication and language as possible. Material needs to be available for highly educated and scientific people, as well as for ordinary citizens of all ages. The effort to publicize, educate, and involve must reach educational institutions as well as media and communications institutions around the globe, perhaps through a network of like-minded organizations that see the need for a whole earth economy. Papers, pamphlets, videos, and Internet-based media will need to be developed for widespread use at conferences, workshops, seminars (conventional and Web-based "webinars"), and study groups.

The task and challenge at this stage is enormous and will require a groundswell of energy, enthusiasm, and conviction of the need to turn away from disaster and toward a whole earth economy. Humans have been able to find this energy before, often for war and conquest but also for cultural and spiritual goals, like the cathedrals of medieval Europe or the push to land on the moon. The goal is to trigger mass appeal for the urgent need to act, so that the demand for change will swell to an overwhelming consensus for a new way forward.

3. *Withdraw from the present system and highlight its illegitimacy.* Nonviolent protest is an exceedingly powerful tool. The boycott of sugar by antislavery campaigners is an example of withdrawal or nonparticipation in the old system. The boycott financially penalized the slaveholders and traders, communicating to the general citizenry the linkage between slavery and their everyday life. Refusing to support the products of slave labor was a way to take morally clear action against slavery. Mohandas Gandhi's salt march against the salt tax in India is another classic example of a well-timed and effective action. It exposed the British system's inequity and venality, while gathering public support from the many who felt empowered by the movement. In search of a catalyst for change, Gandhi created a crisis when one was needed. Today, we have already created for ourselves the biggest crisis ever faced by humanity.

> *Today, we have created for ourselves the biggest crisis ever faced by humanity.*

Henry David Thoreau's one-man act of civil disobedience, refusing to pay war tax, was a small gesture with colossal influence. It inspired Gandhi, who along with Thoreau then inspired Martin Luther King Jr. The Rev. King's nonviolent resistance campaigns for civil rights became a highly effective tool for profound social change. He was followed by Nelson Mandela in South Africa, Lech Wałesa in Poland, and Chico Mendes in Brazil. A chain of people from extremely diverse cultures and societies have passed the moral power of nonviolent resistance onward and through its use have managed to achieve remarkably progressive social, political, and economic goals. The beginnings of the withdrawal of support for the corporate food system, in response to the growing ecological crisis, can be seen in "local food" movements, fair-trade campaigns, and the hundreds of primers and classes now available that teach people how to drastically reduce their ecological footprint.[37]

Those in power who benefit from the current economic order and who rely on manipulation, corruption, and intimidation to retain political control will use all their means to repel the growing message that the present order is illegitimate. But the mounting case for action to build a whole earth economy will gradually weaken the defenses of the power elite, just as it has done in the past in the American South, in colonial India, in the former Soviet Union, and even today in China. Creative protests and withdrawals from reckless, incoherent systems are ways of creating legitimacy and moral authority that can draw more and more participants into action for progressive moral change.

These action items to promote nonviolent reform for building a whole earth economy are overlapping and mutually reinforcing. They are not necessarily sequential, and unforeseen tactical opportunities for action will arise. But tactics have more chance of success in the long run when they fit into an overall strategy. As these plans and actions begin to unfold, champions and political leaders will emerge who will generate more momentum and support. These leaders do not even necessarily have to be outside existing political structures or international organizations. There are progressive leaders and governments that will be eager to support such a program and campaign; think of countries like Norway, states like Kerala in India, and cities like Portland, Oregon, or Curitiba, Brazil.

The analogy of introducing a new computer system in parallel with the old one is once again helpful here. The shift works if professionals develop the new system as much as possible in advance. In the case of new forms of global governance, new or reformed institutions should be conceptually designed and promoted to the maximum, even if the opportunity to implement them is not yet in sight. Unforeseen events—knocks to society's collective head—may suddenly crumble shaky institutions. New openings for new governance models will appear, sometimes suddenly. A bank of well-developed, participatory models and democratic implementation plans ready to go may make the difference between a lurch into social chaos, followed by political authoritarianism, or a transition to cooperative governance for the common good.

It may seem that countries such as the United States, the European Union, China, Russia, Japan, and India, along with the members of the Organization of the Petroleum Exporting Countries, are the most significant players in the global situation. In one sense this is true; yet other countries and international groups can exercise leverage through moral leadership, economic boycotts, and the capacity to influence public opinion. George Monbiot, for example, asks us to ponder the power that all the nations indebted to the IMF would have if they gathered together and refused—all at once—to pay back their debts.[38]

Support for change in global governance may come from many sources, which, if well coordinated, can add up to a powerful movement for the common good. Should concerned citizens wait to react to urgent crises, or should they act on the overwhelming evidence that already exists on the need for a whole earth economy? The answer to that question is abundantly clear: Waiting even a day longer simply does not make sense. The only choice we human beings now have, in terms of survival, is to take immediate action to develop a new platform of everything needed for the big shift, so it will be available to our decision makers when either crisis or mass epiphany forces the fundamental reevaluations that will be necessary.

Call to Action

The scientific community's assessment of global climate change is undeniable: Global warming is happening, and the temperature and sea level are heading rapidly to levels that are harmful to human and other life. Avoiding dangerous increases in temperature is no longer possible. No mitigation effort, regardless how rigorous and relentless, will prevent climate change from happening in the next few decades and centuries. Some form of adaptation is unavoidable. Yet urgent action is needed to prevent a much more catastrophic climate change scenario from overrunning life's adaptive capacities. Unfortunately, climate change is joined by species loss, the disruption of ecosystems on a global scale, vast regional air pollution, ocean acidification, and equally dire events.

The five questions that form the core of this book make this situation crystal clear. The predominant economic system used throughout the planet

- Is incapable of providing an adequate answer to the question: what is the economy *for*?
- Fails to understand how the economy really works
- Is unable to put any boundaries on consumption and waste
- Has no means to even think about fairly distributing both benefits and burdens to present and future generations of people and other species
- Lacks a system of governance that protects life's commonwealth

This state of affairs is allowed to continue because current international governance systems have not evolved to meet the challenges that face us.

Creating the global governance that this book suggests will require enormous societal resources, widespread individual support and participation, and significant institutional reform. This will necessitate strong public pressure. Countries and institutions do not readily give up sovereignty. The overall challenge is to establish a global economic system that is grounded in science and operates in accord with the way the earth works. Meeting this challenge first of all requires research, monitoring, and analysis of the economy's impacts on social and ecological systems. Second, effective global responsibility and protection is needed to ensure the health of essential parts of the earth such as its atmosphere, oceans, and forests. Third, an effective system of mandatory rules and policy management needs to be created for the governance of matters that can only be resolved at a global level. And fourth, effective accountability through judicial functions must accompany policy management and governance.

Creating the global governance that this book suggests will require enormous societal resources, widespread individual support and participation, and significant institutional reform.

The problem at present is that existing global institutions and their capabilities are not functioning in a coherent way within a coordinated policy-management system. No strategic framework of action is guiding international, national, and subnational governance that will ensure the health and well-being of life's commonwealth. Harmonizing the work of current institutions could lead to a pattern of common services and collective decision making that contributes to the attainment of this overall shared goal. In due course, the result could be the creation of institutions such as those envisioned here. This is the way the EU evolved, and the way that new levels of governance systems often emerge.

While the existing patchwork of global agencies might eventually begin to function in a coordinated and coherent manner, it is far from clear that they can, or will, move in this direction. The international community may need to create dramatic new levels of global dialogue, agreement, and institutional structure in order to reform the functional capacities of current institutions into a cohesive design. While it is not possible to foresee exactly how the institutions of global environmental governance will develop, what is clear are the key functions that must come into play and the mandate that calls the earth's peoples to a new kind of politics on behalf of the commonwealth of life.

Changes of such magnitude do not happen easily, and sometimes they do not happen at all. A number of human civilizations have ceased because they did not adapt in time, and destroyed their environment. Radical changes have occurred in times of political, economic, and social crises, often during or at the end of wars.

Some have occurred slowly over decades or centuries. Humankind currently does not have that luxury of slow adaptation.

Do we have to wait for the earth's decline to reach such a crisis point that it can no longer support significant numbers of people and species, before we unite with our fellow human beings to bring about the necessary economic and governance changes? If we do wait, widespread environmental degradation and escalating violent conflict over energy, water, wood, and food are inevitable, with even larger and more tragic population movements than the planet is already enduring. Many people will die, and many will endure lives of great misery.

Urgent action is needed *now* to avoid reacting to crises of this magnitude. The task for people who are concerned for human survival and the welfare of the commonwealth of life is to help bring awareness of the connections between the looming ecological threats and the political and governance changes needed to avoid them, and to join together to persuade political leaders and parties to act. Protest movements using nonviolent means have yielded enduring results in the past.

Economic and governance changes are necessary for building a whole earth economy, but a more profound new direction is also required. This more fundamental change is a values change. Instead of the anxious, illusory pursuit of more money and possessions, people need to think about pursuing joyful, grateful, and fulfilling lives in right relationship with life's commonwealth. Values progression of this kind is needed not only at a personal level but also in institutions and enterprises at the community, national, and international level. Many indigenous peoples already have cultural values and belief systems that support right relationships, which rest primarily on respect and gratitude for all that is.

It is sadly ironic that so-called "developed countries" urgently need to learn basic survival skills, including how to enjoy life within the finite reality of this planet's resource limits, from "undeveloped" peoples to whom Western ideas of advancement have brought so much loss. But taking inspiration from indigenous peoples and others who have learned how to live joyfully in right relationship with the earth is the key to the long-term survival of life as we know it.

The guidance system of right relationship needs to be reflected in laws, professional rules, organizational charters, policies, codes of conduct, creeds, and religious doctrines. It can arise in cultural customs and through myths, stories, and traditions. For some people, the change will be through a spiritual epiphany, while others will walk different paths. Which path is not important, as long as it leads to the changes needed to build a whole earth economy . . . *If we have time.*

> *People need to think about pursuing joyful, grateful, and fulfilling lives in right relationship with life's commonwealth.*

Notes

Preface

1. Philips P. Moulton, ed., *The Journal and Major Essays of John Woolman* (Richmond, VA: Friends United, 1989).

2. Boulding described the earth as a spaceship as follows:

"In the imagination of those who are sensitive to the realities of our era, the earth has become a space ship, and this, perhaps, is the most important single fact of our day. . . . It is not only that man's image of the earth has changed; the reality of the world social system has changed. . . .

The consequences of earth becoming a space ship for the social system are profound and little understood. It is clear that much human behavior and many human institutions in the past, which were appropriate to a [seemingly] infinite earth, are entirely inappropriate to small closed space ship.

The closed earth of the future requires economic principles which are somewhat different from those of the open earth of the past. . . . I am tempted to call the open economy the "cowboy economy," the cowboy being symbolic of the illimitable plains and also associated with reckless, exploitative, romantic, and violent behavior. . . . The closed economy of the future might similarly be called the "spaceman" economy, in which the earth has become a single space ship without unlimited reservoirs of anything, either for extraction or pollution . . .

Man is finally going to have to face the fact that he is a biological system living in an ecological system, and that his survival power is going to depend on his developing symbiotic relationships of a closed cycle character with all the other element and populations of the world of ecological systems."

"Earth as a Space Ship," a presentation made to the Committee on Space Sciences, Washington State University, on May 10, 1965: Kenneth Boulding Papers, Archives (Box #38), University of Colorado at Boulder Libraries. "The Economics of the Coming Spaceship Earth," in *Environmental Quality in a Growing Society* (Baltimore, MD: Johns Hopkins University Press, 1966), pp. 253 ff.

Introduction

1. Peter Woodford, "Health Canada Muzzles Oils Sands Whistleblower," *National Review of Medicine* 4, no. 6 (March 30, 2007): 2; Christopher Hatch and Matt Price, *Canada's Toxic Tar Sands: The Most Destructive Project on Earth* (Toronto: Environmental Defence, February 2008), www.environmentaldefence.ca/reports/pdf/TarSands_TheReport.pdf (accessed June 1, 2008).

2. Aldo Leopold, *A Sand County Almanac* (New York: Oxford University Press, 1949), 224–25.

3. Albert Schweitzer, *Out of My Life and Thought* (New York: Henry Holt, 1933), 186–88.

4. Millennium Ecosystem Assessment, "Guide to the Millennium Assessment Reports," www.millenniumassessment.org/en/index.aspx (accessed June 26, 2008).

5. Robert Kuttner, *The Squandering of America: How the Failure of Our Politics Undermines Our Prosperity* (New York: Knopf, 2007).

6. This is the basic principle of ecological economics. See generally, for example, works by Herman Daly and Robert Costanza.

7. Nicholas Georgescu-Roegen, *The Entropy Law and the Economic Process* (Cambridge, MA: Harvard University Press, 1971), 220–23.

8. Stefan Baumgärtner and others, "Joint Production," *Internet Encyclopaedia of Ecological Economics*, International Society of Ecological Economics (February 2003).

9. William McDonough and Michael Braungart, *Cradle to Cradle: Remaking the Way We Make Things* (New York: North Point, 2002).

10. Herman Daly, *Beyond Growth: The Economics of Sustainable Development* (Boston: Beacon, 1996), 31-44.

11. Paul R. Ehrlich and John P. Holdren, "Impact of Population Growth," *Science* 171, no. 3977 (1971): 1212–17.

12. Kenneth Boulding, "Love and Lifeboats" (chapel talk, Gustavus Adolphus College, St. Peter, MN, November 18, 1975), www.colorado.edu/econ/Kenneth.Boulding/quotes/q.body.21.html (accessed June 26, 2008).

13. Global Issues, "Causes of Poverty," www.globalissues.org/TradeRelated/Facts.asp (accessed June 26, 2008).

14. Perry Anderson, "Depicting Europe," *London Review of Books* 29, no. 18 (2007), www.lrb.co.uk/v29/n18/ande01_.html (accessed June 26, 2008).

Chapter 1: What's the Economy For?
A Flourishing Commonwealth of Life

1. *Epigraph*. Robert Skidelsky, *John Maynard Keynes: The Economist as Savior 1920–37* (New York: Viking Penguin, 1994), xxiii.

2. The background for this discussion can be found in two modern classics of political economy: Karl Polanyi, *The Great Transformation: The Political and Economic Origins of Our Time* (Boston: Beacon Press, 1957); and Ellen Meiksins Wood, *The Origin of Capitalism: A Longer View* (London: Verso, 2002).

3. Robert Lekachman, *The Age of Keynes: The Life, Times, Thought and Triumph of the Greatest Economist of Our Age* (New York: Random House, 1966).

4. The standard assumptions include perfect competition, no externalities, and accurate information, and apply only to private goods, such as automobiles, not public ones, like clean air.

5. Peter G. Brown, *Restoring the Public Trust: Fresh Vision for Progressive Government in the United States* (Boston: Beacon Press, 1994), 49–66 for why the theory of market failures itself fails as a theory of government legitimacy.

6. Robert H. Nelson, *Reaching for Heaven on Earth: The Theological Meaning of Economics* (New York: Littlefield Adams, 1993); *Economics as Religion: From Samuelson to Chicago and Beyond* (State College: Pennsylvania State University Press, 2001).

7. Peter Victor, *Managing Without Growth* (Cheltenham, UK: Edward Elgar, 2008).

8. Walter K. Dodds, *Humanity's Footprint: Momentum, Impact, and Our Global Environment* (New York: Columbia University Press, 2008), 111.

9. Lewis Mumford, *The Transformations of Man* (New York: Harper & Row, 1956).

10. Paul Raskin and others, *Great Transition: The Promise and Lure of the Times Ahead* (Boston: Stockholm Environment Institute, 2002), www.tellus.org/Documents/Great_Transitions.pdf (accessed June 26, 2008).

11. Melissa K. Nelson, *Original Instructions: Indigenous Teachings for a Sustainable Future* (Rochester, VT: Bear, 2008).

12. Jean Briggs, *Never in Anger: Portrait of an Eskimo Family* (Cambridge, MA: Harvard University Press, 1970).

13. Stephen Ambrose, *Undaunted Courage: Meriwether Lewis, Thomas Jefferson, and the Opening of the American West* (New York: Simon & Schuster, 1997).

14. Jonathan Lear, *Radical Hope: Ethics in the Face of Cultural Devastation* (Cambridge, MA: Harvard University Press, 2006).

15. Pare Lorentz, Dir., *The Plow That Broke the Plains* (U.S. Resettlement Administration, 1936), documentary film.

Chapter 2: How Does It Work?
Putting the Economy in Its Place

1. Erwin Schrödinger, *What Is Life?* (Cambridge: Cambridge University Press, 1967).

2. James Gustave Speth, *The Bridge at the Edge of the World: Capitalism, the Environment, and Crossing from Crisis to Sustainability* (New Haven, CT: Yale University Press, 2008), 37–38.

3. Thomas Berry and Brian Swimme, *The Universe Story: From the Primordial Flaring Forth to the Ecozoic Era* (New York: Harper & Row, 1994).

4. Thomas Berry, *The Great Work: Our Way into the Future* (New York: Bell Tower, 1999).

5. Stuart Kauffman, *At Home in the Universe: The Search for the Laws of Self-Organization and Complexity* and *Investigations* (New York: Oxford University Press, 1995).

6. Lynn Margulis, *Microcosmos: Four Billion Years of Evolution from Our Microbial Ancestors* (Berkeley: University of California Press, 1986).

7. Eric Chaisson, *The Life Era: Cosmic Selection and Conscious Evolution* (Lincoln, NE: iUniverse.com,1987).

8. Fritjof Capra, *The Hidden Connections: Integrating the Biological, Cognitive, and Social Dimensions of Life into a Science of Sustainability* (New York: Doubleday, 2002).

9. Melissa K. Nelson, *Original Instructions: Indigenous Teachings for a Sustainable Future* (Rochester, VT: Bear, 2008).

10. Center for the Study of World Religions, Harvard Divinity School, www.hds.harvard.edu/cswr/ (accessed June 26, 2008).

11. Michel Serres, *The Natural Contract* and *Genesis* (Ann Arbor: University of Michigan Press, 1995).

12. Thomas Berry, *The Great Work: Our Way into the Future* (New York: Bell Tower, 1999).

13. In the second half of the twentieth century, the field of environmental ethics blossomed. Two of the most promising people in that field are Bryan Norton and Paul Taylor. But many authors failed to engage seriously with evolutionary biology and ecology.

14. Albert Schweitzer, *Out of My Life and Thought* (New York: Henry Holt, 1933), 185.

15. Aldo Leopold, *A Sand County Almanac* (New York: Oxford University Press, 1949).

16. Leopold, *A Sand County Almanac*, 224–25.

17. The highly significant work of architect William McDonough and his associates in pioneering the use and reuse of "cradle-to-cradle" materials in manufacturing are examples of this kind of thinking. The book *Cradle to Cradle*, which he cowrote, is now a classic in this rapidly emerging field of industrial design and manufacturing planning. William McDonough and Michael Braungart, *Cradle to Cradle: Remaking the Way We Make Things* (New York: North Point, 2002).

18. Karl-Henrik Robèrt, *The Natural Step Story: Seeding a Quiet Revolution* (Gabriola Island, BC: New Society, 2008).

19. Some of the companies using the Natural Step methodology include Ikea, Electrolux, Nike, Starbucks, Du Pont, Alcan, and The Co-operators. See Natural Step Society, "The Natural Step," www.naturalstep.ca (accessed June 26, 2008).

20. See page vii.

Chapter 3: How Big Is Too Big?
Boundaries on Consumption and Waste

1. *Epigraph.* James Gustave Speth, *The Bridge at the Edge of the World: Capitalism, the Environment, and Crossing from Crisis to Sustainability* (New Haven, CT: Yale University Press, 2008), x.

2. Economists and others initially considered the impacts of re-source scarcity on economic growth, with the initial prevailing view that "resource scarcity did not yet, and probably would not soon, and conceiv-ably might not ever, halt growth." More recently, the concept of a "new scarcity" that examines the limits on ecological systems to handle waste, ecosystem loss, pollution, greenhouse gases, and so on has been recog-nized as being of paramount importance. R. D. Simpson, M. A. Toman, and R. U. Ayres, eds., *Scarcity and Growth Revisited: Natural Resources and the Environment in the New Millennium* (Washington, DC: Resources for the Future, 2005), 1 (discussing Harold J. Barnett and Chandler Morse, *Scarcity and Growth* [Washington, DC: RFF, 1965]).

3. One prominent assessment is NASA scientist James Hansen's view that humans have approximately one decade to take action that will limit the rise in the earth's average temperature to 2°C from preindustrial levels, which he believes is necessary to avoid the catastrophe associated with a 5°C increase, which would "transform the planet and would be disastrous for humans and other species." See Jim Hansen, "The Threat to the Planet: An Exchange," *New York Review of Books* 53, no. 12 (2006), www.nybooks.com/articles/19131 (accessed June 26, 2008).

4. Speth's *Bridge at the End of the World* opens with a startling array of graphs showing these trend lines (in unnumbered pages preceding the Introduction).

5. Millennium Ecosystem Assessment, "Guide to the Millennium Assessment Reports," www.millenniumassessment.org/en/index.aspx (ac-cessed June 26, 2008).

6. Ibid.

7. Jared Diamond, "Environmental Collapse and the End of Civil-ization," *Harpers*, June 2003, 43.

8. Brian Walker and David Salt, *Resilience Thinking: Sustaining Ecosystems and People in a Changing World* (Washington, DC: Island Press, 2006), 75.

9. Walker and Salt, *Resilience Thinking*, 59, 62.

10. J. Baird Callicott and Eric T. Freyfogle, eds., *Aldo Leopold: For the Health of the Land* (Washington, DC: Island Press, 1999), 219. Leopold describes the symptoms of land sickness as follows: "They include abnormal erosion, abnormal intensity of floods, decline of yields in crops and forests, decline of carrying capacity in pastures and ranges, outbreak of some species as pests and the disappearance of others without visible cause, a general tendency toward the shortening of species lists and food chains, and a world-wide dominance of plant and animal weeds." We are grateful to Baird Callicott for assisting us in our understanding of Leopold's idea of beauty.

11. Lewis Mumford, *The Culture of Cities* (Orlando, FL: Harvest, 1970).

12. Jane Jacobs, *The Death and Life of Great American Cities* (New York: Random House, 1961).

13. Charles Darwin, *Origin of Species* (New York: Signet Classics, 2003), chapter 14.

14. Paul R. Ehrlich and John P. Holdren, "Impact of Population Growth," *Science* 171, no. 3977 (1971): 1212–17.

15. Eugene A. Rosa, Richard York, and Thomas Dietz, "Footprints on the Earth: The Environmental Consequences of Modernity," *American Sociological Review*, April 2003, 279–97.

16. International Institute for Applied Systems Analysis, World Population Program, "2007 update of probabilistic world population projections," www.iiasa.ac.at/Research/POP/proj07 (accessed June 26, 2008).

17. Simpson, Toman, and Ayres, *Scarcity and Growth Revisited*, 6.

18. Enunciated in 1865 by William Stanley Jevons in his book *The Coal Question*.

19. George Monbiot, *Heat* (Toronto: Doubleday, 2006), 61. The Jevons Paradox is discussed in regard to how more efficient use of coal increased coal use overall and helped fuel the industrial revolution.

20. Barbara Kingsolver, *Animal, Vegetable, Miracle* (New York: HarperCollins, 2007).

Chapter 4: What's Fair? Sharing Life's Bounty

1.   The Universal Declaration of Human Rights is part of what is informally called the International Bill of Rights, whose other two components are the International Covenant on Civil and Political Rights and the International Covenant on Economic, Social, and Cultural Rights. The two covenants, completed in 1966, became international law in 1976 after a sufficient number of countries ratified them (though not, notably, the United States, which never ratified the latter covenant).

2.   John Rawls, *A Theory of Justice* (Cambridge, MA: Harvard University Press, 1971), 302.

3.   While acknowledging the great contribution of the work, to date, on ecological footprinting, the authors view this emerging assessment tool as a work in progress. As an overall measure of ecological impact, it both understates and overstates impact in important ways that require further study and refinement.

4.   Personal communication between Peter G. Brown and Wes Jackson, president of the Land Institute, Salinas, Kansas.

5.   Lester Thurow, "Income Distribution as a Pure Public Good," *Quarterly Journal of Economics* (1971): 327–36.

6.   National Oceanic and Atmospheric Administration, "Restoration Economics: Discounting and Time Preference," NOAA Coastal Services Center, www.csc.noaa.gov/coastal/economics/discounting.htm (accessed June 26, 2008).

Chapter 5: Governance: New Ways to Stay in Bounds and Play Fair

1.   Geoff Garver, "Tooth Decay," *The Environmental Forum* 25, no. 3 (2008): 34–39.

2.   *National Environmental Policy Act*, U.S. Code 43 (1969), § 4331.

3.   World Wildlife Fund, "Living Planet Report," www.panda.org/news_facts/publications/living_planet_report/index.cfm (accessed June 26, 2008).

4.   Ibid.

5.   Al Gore, *An Inconvenient Truth: The Planetary Emergency of Global Warming and What We Can Do About It* (New York: Rodale, 2006).

6. Frank Biermann and Steffen Bauer, eds., *A World Environment Organization: Solution or Threat for Effective International Environmental Governance* (Burlington, VT: Ashgate, 2005), 3.

7. Frank Biermann, "Global Governance and the Environment," in *International Environmental Politics*, ed. M. Betsill, K. Hochstetler, and D. Stevis (New York: Palgrave MacMillan, 2005); Mark Imber, "United Nations Environment Programme," in *International Encyclopedia of Environmental Politics*, ed. John Barry and E. Gene Frankland (New York: Routledge, 2002); David Held in *Debating Globalization*, ed. Anthony Barnett, David Held, and Caspar Henderson, (Cambridge, UK: Polity, 2005).

8. Hubert Reeves and Frédéric Lenoir, *Mal de Terre* (Paris: Seuil, 2003), 50–55.

9. Earth Charter International Secretariat, "The Earth Charter Initiative," www.earthcharter.org (accessed June 26, 2008).

10. Colin Soskolne, ed., *Sustaining Life on Earth: Environmental and Human Health Through Global Governance* (Lanham, MD: Lexington, 2007).

11. The Global Footprint Network is developing ways to use ecological footprinting to develop standards. Global Footprint Network, *Ecological Footprint Standards 2006*, www.footprintstandards.org (accessed June 26, 2008). For an independent critique of ecological footprinting, noting its strengths and weaknesses, see Aaron Best and others. "Potential of the Ecological Footprint for monitoring environmental impacts from natural resource use: Analysis of the potential of the Ecological Footprint and related assessment tools for use in the EU's Thematic Strategy on the Sustainable Use of Natural Resources," May 2008. Report to the European Commission, DG Environment. http://ec.europa.eu/environment/natres/pdf/footprint.pdf.

12. "[C]ompanies spend billions of dollars making sure you know about their product. In 2001 on direct media advertising alone, that's radio, television, and print, McDonald's spent $1.4 billion worldwide getting you to buy their products. On direct media advertising Pepsi spent more than $1 billion. To advertise its candy Hershey Foods spent almost $200 million. In its peak year, the five-a-day fruit and vegetable campaign had a total advertising budget, in all media, of just $2 million—100 times less than just the direct media budget of one candy company. We are

being bombarded by the food industry with lies, deceptions, and brain-washing, getting us to believe their products are healthy and good for us—and it's working. Think about the way food is marketed: tee shirts, coupons, toys for children, giveaways in fast-food places, and placemats, and all the different ways to get you to buy food. The most heavily advertised foods are the most consumed. There is no surprise. Whoever spends the most money on advertising sells the most food." Natural Cures, "Questions About Healthy Foods, Diets and Cleanses," www.naturalcures.com/NC/faq3.aspx (accessed June 26, 2008).

13. Stiftung Warentest, "Stiftung Warentest," www.test.de (accessed June 26, 2008).

14. Evangelical Environmental Network, "What Would Jesus Drive?" www.whatwouldjesusdrive.org (accessed June 26, 2008).

15. Richard Musgrave, *The Theory of Public Finance* (New York: McGraw Hill, 1959).

16. Reeves and Lenoir, *Mal de Terre*.

17. I. de Vegh, "The International Clearing Union," *The American Economic Review* 33, no. 3 (1943): 534–56.

18. James S. Henry, *The Blood Bankers: Tales from the Global Underground Economy* (New York: Four Walls Eight Windows, 2003); Joseph E. Stiglitz, *Globalization and Its Discontents* (New York: W. W. Norton, 2002); David C. Korten, *When Corporations Rule the World* (San Francisco: Berrett-Koehler, 1995).

19. David Keith Goodin helped the authors in developing the idea of the ICU as a means to ecological stability.

20. Global Environment Facility, "Project Database," http://gefonline.org.

21. Peter Barnes, *Who Owns the Sky? Our Common Assets and the Future of Capitalism* (Washington, DC: Island, 2001), and *Capitalism 3.0: A Guide to Reclaiming the Commons* (San Francisco: Berrett-Koehler, 2006).

22. Peter Barnes cites the Alaska Permanent Fund, which distributes oil revenues to each citizen on a per capita basis, as an example of his idea already in practice. But he does not emphasize that this has undercut the ability of Alaska to restrict oil development, because the citizens get paid more when there is more development.

23. A guaranteed global income is not the sole option. For instance, the trustees could set up a universal literacy and numeracy fund so that all people who wished to be able to read and do arithmetic would be able to do so.

24. Andrew Strauss, "Overcoming the Dysfunction of the Bifurcated Global System: The Promise of a People's Assembly," in *Reframing the International: Law, Culture, Politics*, ed. Richard Falk, Lester Edwin Ruiz, R. B. J. Walker (New York: Routledge, 2002).

25. George Monbiot, *The Age of Consent: Manifesto for a New World Order* (London: Harper Perennial, 2003).

26. Myron J. Frankman, *World Democratic Federalism: Peace and Justice Indivisible* (New York: Palgrave MacMillan, 2004).

27. Perry Anderson, "Depicting Europe," *London Review of Books* 29, no. 18 (2007), www.lrb.co.uk/v29/n18/ande01_.html (accessed June 26, 2008).

28. J. A. Chandler, *Local Government Today* (Manchester, UK: Manchester University Press, 1996), and ed., *Local Government in Liberal Democracies* (New York: Routledge, 1993).

29. James MacGregor Burns and others, eds., *State and Local Politics: Government by the People*, 9th ed. (Upper Saddle River, NJ: Prentice Hall, 1998).

30. Wolf Linder, *Swiss Democracy* (New York: St. Martin's, 1994).

31. George Orwell, *Nineteen Eighty-Four* (London: Plume, 1983).

32. Garrett Hardin, "The Tragedy of the Commons," *Science* 162 (1968): 1243–48.

33. George Monbiot, "The Tragedy of Enclosure," www.monbiot.com/ archives/1994/01/01/the-tragedy-of-enclosure (accessed June 26, 2008).

34. Adirondack Park Agency, "Adirondack Park Agency," www.apa .state.ny.us (accessed June 26, 2008).

35. Jim Merkel, *Radical Simplicity* (Gabriola Island, BC: New Society, 2003), 189.

Conclusion

1. Mary Catherine Bateson, *Our Own Metaphor* (New York: Alfred A. Knopf, 1972), 12–13.

2. Paul Hawken, *Blessed Unrest: How the Largest Movement in the World Came into Being and Why No One Saw It Coming* (New York: Viking, 2007).

3. While much of this research is science based and appears in technical journals, a variety of books for the general reader have made this "big history" readily available. Here are some notable examples: David Christian, *Maps of Time: An Introduction to Big History* (Berkeley: University of California Press, 2004); Richard Fortey, *Earth: An Intimate History* (New York: Alfred A. Knopf, 2004); Michael Novacek, *Terra: Our 100-Million-Year-Old Ecosystem—and the Threats That Now Put It at Risk* (New York: Farrar, Straus, and Giroux, 2007); Tim Flannery, *The Eternal Frontier: An Ecological History of North America and Its Peoples* (New York: Grove, 2001); J. R. McNeill, *Something New Under the Sun: An Environmental History of the Twentieth-Century World* (New York: W. W. Norton, 2000).

4. Doug Struck, "NOAA Scientists Say Arctic Ice Is Melting Faster Than Expected," *Washington Post*, Sept. 7, 2007, page A06.

5. Jared Diamond, Collapse: *How Societies Choose to Fail or Succeed* (New York: Viking, 2005).

6. Ibid., 421.

7. According to recent news reports, the Chinese are seriously considering changes in their population control policies, in response to the perception, prevalent in many other regions, that a rise in birth rate is needed to support an aging population. See, for example, Jim Yardley, "China to Reconsider One-Child Limit," *New York Times*, Feb. 29, 2008.

8. Berlin University, "Dahlem Konferenzen," Berlin, www.fu-berlin.de/veranstaltungen/dahlemkonferenzen/en/index.htm (accessed June 1, 2008).

9. Hans Joachim Schellnhuber and others, eds., *Earth System Analysis for Sustainability* (Cambridge, MA: MIT Press, 2004); Robert Costanza, Lisa J. Graumlich, and Will Steffen, eds., *Sustainability or Collapse? An Integrated History and Future of People on Earth* (Cambridge, MA: MIT Press, 2007).

10. James Lovelock, *The Revenge of Gaia: Earth's Climate Crisis and the Fate of Humanity* (New York: Basic Books, 2006).

11. Earth Charter International Secretariat, "Earth Charter in Action," http://earthcharterinaction.org/about_charter.html.

12. International Union of Conservation and Nature, "IUCN," http://cms.iucn.org.

13. Ibid.

14. Stern Review on the Economics of Climate Change, www.hm-treasury.gov.uk/independent_reviews/stern_review_economics_climate_change/stern_review_Report.cfm (accessed June 26, 2008).

15. Researchers include Eugene Rosa, Richard York, and Thomas Dietz, "Footprints on the Earth: The Environmental Consequences of Modernity," *American Sociological Review*, April 2003; Barry Commoner, Michael Corr, and Paul J. Stamler, "The Causes of Pollution," *Environment* 13 (1971): 2–19.

16. Aaron Best and others. "Potential of the Ecological Footprint for monitoring environmental impacts from natural resource use: Analysis of the potential of the Ecological Footprint and related assessment tools for use in the EU's Thematic Strategy on the Sustainable Use of Natural Resources," May 2008. Report to the European Commission, DG Environment. http://ec.europa.eu/environment/natres/pdf/footprint.pdf.

17. Millennium Ecosystem Assessment, www.millennium-assessment.org/en/index.aspx (accessed June 26, 2008).

18. Jim Merkel, *Radical Simplicity* (Gabriola Island, BC: New Society, 2003), 26–44.

19. Ibid.

20. Peter Barnes, *Who Owns the Sky? Our Common Assets and the Future of Capitalism* (Washington, DC: Island Press, 2001), and *Capitalism 3.0: A Guide to Reclaiming the Commons* (San Francisco: Berrett-Koehler, 2006).

21. Richard Falk, in *Global Governance Reader*, ed. Rorden Wilkenson (New York: Routledge, 2005), 124, 128.

22. Robert Keohane, in *Global Governance Reader*, ed. Rorden Wilkenson (New York: Routledge, 2005).

23. George Monbiot, *The Age of Consent: Manifesto for a New World Order* (London: Harper Perennial, 2003).

24. "Call the Blue Helmets," *The Economist*, Jan. 4, 2007, www.uiowa.edu/~c030060/ecst.peacekeeping.htm (accessed June 26, 2008). (Emphasis added.)

25. Deepak Nayyar, ed., *Governing Globalization: Issues and Institutions* (Oxford: Oxford University Press, 2002), 360.

26. Peter Victor, *Managing Without Growth* (Cheltenham, UK: Edward Elgar, 2008).

27. Henry David Thoreau, "Resistance to Civil Government," in *Walden and Resistance to Civil Government*, ed. William Ross (New York: W. W. Norton, 1992), 244.

28. Adam Hochschild, *Bury the Chains: Prophets and Rebels in the Fight to Free an Empire's Slaves* (Boston: Houghton-Mifflin, 2004).

29. "Breaking the Chains," *The Economist*, Feb. 24, 2007, www .economist.com/world/international/displaystory.cfm?story_id= E1RSQJQDG (accessed June 26, 2008); V. A. C. Gatrell, *The Hanging Tree: Execution and the English People 1770–1868* (New York: Oxford University Press, 1996), 396–403.

30. Ibid.

31. Intergovernmental Panel on Climate Change, "IPCC Reports," www.ipcc.ch/ipccreports/index.htm (accessed June 26, 2008).

32. United Nations Environment Programme, "UNEP Publi-cations," www.unep.org/publications (accessed June 26, 2008).

33. Worldwatch Institute, "State of the World," www.worldwatch.org/ taxonomy/term/38 (accessed June 26, 2008).

34. World Wildlife Fund, "Living Planet Report," www.panda.org/ news_facts/publications/living_planet_report/index.cfm (accessed June 26, 2008).

35. Pugwash Online, "The Pugwash Conferences," www.pugwash.org (accessed June 26, 2008).

36. Global Ecological Integrity Group, "Global Ecological Integrity Group," www.globalecointegrity.net (accessed June 26, 2008).

37. Barbara Kingsolver, *Animal, Vegetable, Miracle* (New York: HarperCollins, 2007); William McKibben, *Deep Economy* (New York: Henry Holt, 2007); Merkel, *Radical Simplicity*.

38. Monbiot, *The Age of Consent*.

Resources

Ackerman, Peter, and Jack DuVall. *A Force More Powerful: A Century of Non-violent Conflict.* New York: St. Martin's, 2000.

Allen, Paula Gunn. *The Sacred Hoop: Recovering the Feminine in American Indian Traditions.* Boston: Beacon, 1992.

Anielski, Mark. *The Economics of Happiness: Building Genuine Wealth.* Gabriola Island, BC: New Society, 2007.

Athanasiou, Tom. *Divided Planet: The Ecology of Rich and Poor.* Athens: University of Georgia Press, 1998.

Attfield, Robin. *Environmental Ethics: An Overview for the Twenty-First Century.* Cambridge: Polity, 2003.

Barnes, Peter. *Capitalism 3.0: A Guide to Reclaiming the Commons.* San Francisco: Berrett-Koehler, 2006.

———. *Who Owns the Sky? Our Common Assets and the Future of Capitalism.* Washington, DC: Island, 2001.

Beck, Ulrich. *World Risk Society.* Cambridge: Polity, 1998.

Bernstein, Jared. *All Together Now: Common Sense for a Fair Economy.* San Francisco: Berrett-Koehler, 2006.

Berry, Thomas, and Brian Swimme. *The Universe Story: From the Primordial Flaring Forth to the Ecozoic Era.* New York: Harper & Row, 1994.

Bollier, David. *Silent Theft: The Private Plunder of Our Common Wealth.* New York: Routledge, 2003.

Booth, Ken, Tim Dunne, and Michael Cox, eds. *How Might We Live: Global Ethics in the New Century.* Cambridge: Cambridge University Press, 2001.

Boulding, Elise. *Building a Global Culture.* Syracuse, NY: Syracuse University Press, 1988.

Boulding, Elise, and Kenneth Boulding. *The Future: Images and Process.* Thousand Oaks, CA: Sage, 1995.

Boulding, Kenneth E. *Economics as a Science.* Lanham, MD: University Press of America,1988.

———. *The Image: Knowledge in Life and Society.* Ann Arbor: University of Michigan Press, 1965.

———. *The Meaning of the Twentieth Century: The Great Transition.* New York: Harper & Row, 1964.

Bozeman, Barry. *Public Values and Public Interest: Counterbalancing Economic Individualism.* Washington, DC: Georgetown University Press, 2007.

Brinton, Howard H., and Margaret Hope Bacon. *Friends for 300 Years: The History and Beliefs of the Society of Friends Since George Fox Started the Quaker Movement.* Wallingford, PA: Pendle Hill, 1965.

Brown, Lester. *Plan B 3.0: Mobilizing to Save Civilization.* New York: W. W. Norton, 2008.

Brown, Peter G. *The Commonwealth of Life: Economics for a Flourishing Earth.* Montreal: Black Rose Books, 2008.

———. *Restoring the Public Trust: A Fresh Vision for Progressive Government in America.* Boston: Beacon, 1994.

Callicott, J. Baird. "The Search for an Environmental Ethic." In *Matters of Life and Death*, edited by T. Regan, 381–424. Toronto: McGraw-Hill, 1992.

Carse, James P. *Finite and Infinite Games: A Vision of Life as Play and Possibility.* New York: Free Press, 1986.

Cavanagh, John, and Jerry Mander, eds. *Alternatives to Economic Globalization: A Better World Is Possible.* San Francisco: Berrett-Koehler, 2002.

Chaisson, Eric. *Epic of Evolution: Seven Ages of the Cosmos.* New York: Columbia University Press, 2006.

Costanza, Robert, Lisa J. Graumlich, and Will Steffen, eds. *Sustainability or Collapse? An Integrated History and Future of People on Earth.* Cambridge, MA: MIT Press, 2007.

Daly, Herman. *Beyond Growth: The Economics of Sustainable Development.* Boston: Beacon, 1996.

———. *Ecological Economics and Sustainable Development.* Chelten-ham, UK: Edward Elgar, 2008.

———. *Steady-State Economics.* 2nd ed. Washington, DC: Island, 1991.

Daly, Herman E., and John B. Cobb Jr. *For the Common Good: Redirecting the Economy Toward Community, the Environment, and a Sustainable Future.* Boston: Beacon, 1989.

Daly, Herman E., and Joshua Farley. *Ecological Economics: Principles and Applications.* Washington, DC: Island, 2004.

Diamond, Jared. *Collapse: How Societies Choose to Fail or Succeed.* New York: Viking, 2005.

Dodds, Walter K. *Humanity's Footprint: Momentum, Impact, and Our Global Environment.* New York: Columbia University Press, 2008.

Douthwaite, Richard. *The Growth Illusion: How Economic Growth Has Enriched the Few, Impoverished the Many, and Endangered the Planet.* 2nd ed. Gabriola Island, BC: New Society, 1999.

Ehrlich, Paul R., and Anne Ehrlich. *One with Nineveh: Politics, Consumption, and the Human Future.* Washington, DC: Island, 2004.

Ekins, Paul. *Economic Growth and Environmental Sustainability.* New York: Routledge, 2000.

Falk, Richard. *Predatory Globalization.* Cambridge: Polity, 1999.

Finn, Daniel K. *The Moral Ecology of Markets: Assessing Claims about Markets and Justice.* Cambridge: Cambridge University Press, 2006.

Foley, Duncan K. *Adam's Fallacy: A Guide to Economic Theology.* Cambridge, MA: Harvard University Press, 2006.

Fullbrook, Edward, ed. *A Guide to What's Wrong with Economics.* London: Anthem, 2004.

Galbraith, John Kenneth. *American Capitalism: The Concept of Countervailing Power.* New York: Houghton Mifflin, 1962.

Gardner, Gary. *Inspiring Progress: Religions' Contribution to Sustainable Development.* New York: W. W. Norton, 2006.

George, Susan. *The Lugano Report: On Preserving Capitalism in the Twenty-First Century.* 2nd ed. London: Pluto, 2003.

Georgescu-Roegen, Nicholas. *The Entropy Law and Economic Process.* Cambridge, MA: Harvard University Press, 1971.

Gibson-Graham, J. K. *The End of Capitalism (As We Knew It): A Feminist Critique of Political Economy.* 2nd ed. Minneapolis: University of Minnesota Press, 2006.

Glyn, Andrew. *Capitalism Unleashed: Finance, Globalization, and Welfare.* New York: Oxford University Press, 2006.

Gunderson, Lance, and C. S. Holling. *Panarchy: Understanding Transformations in Human and Natural Systems.* Washington, DC: Island, 2002.

Hamilton, Clive. *Growth Fetish.* London: Pluto, 2004.

Hawken, Paul, Amory Lovins, and L. Hunter Lovins. *Natural Capitalism: Creating the Next Industrial Revolution.* Boston: Little, Brown, 1999.

Heinberg, Richard. *The Party's Over: Oil, War, and the Fate of Industrial Societies.* Gabriola Island, BC: New Society, 2003.

Henson, Robert. *The Rough Guide to Climate Change.* New York: Rough Guides, 2006.

Hick, John. *The Fifth Dimension.* Oxford: Oneworld, 1999.

Jamieson, Dale. *Morality's Progress: Essays on Humans, Other Animals, and the Rest of Nature.* Oxford: Oxford University Press, 2002.

Keen, Steve. *Debunking Economics: The Naked Emperor of the Social Sciences.* London: Zed Books, 2001.

Kelly, Marjorie. *The Divine Right of Capital: Dethroning the Corporate Aristocracy.* San Francisco: Berrett-Koehler, 2003.

Kingsolver, Barbara. *Animal, Vegetable, Miracle.* New York: Harper-Collins, 2007.

Kitching, Gavin. *Seeking Social Justice through Globalization: Escaping a Nationalist Perspective.* State College: Pennsylvania State University Press, 2001.

Knight, Richard, and Suzanne Riedel, eds. *Aldo Leopold and the Ecological Conscience.* Oxford: Oxford University Press, 2002.

Korten, David C. *The Great Turning: From Empire to Earth Community.* San Francisco: Berrett-Koehler, 2006.

Krugman, Paul. *The Conscience of a Liberal.* New York: W. W. Norton, 2007.

Kuttner, Robert. *The Squandering of America: How the Failure of Our Politics Undermines Our Prosperity.* New York: Alfred Knopf, 2007.

Laidi, Zaki. *The Great Disruption.* Cambridge: Polity, 2007.

Lakoff, George, and Mark Johnson. *Philosophy in the Flesh: The Embodied Mind and Its Challenge to Western Thought.* New York: Basic Books, 1999.

Leopold, Aldo. *A Sand County Almanac.* New York: Oxford University Press, 1949.

Linder, Wolf. *Swiss Democracy.* New York: St. Martin's, 1994.

Lovejoy, Thomas E., and Lee Hannah, eds. *Climate Change and Biodiversity.* New Haven, CT: Yale University Press, 2005.

Lovelock, James. *The Revenge of Gaia: Earth's Climate Crisis and the Fate of Humanity.* New York: Basic Books, 2006.

Lynas, Mark. *Six Degrees: Our Future on a Hotter Planet.* New York: Harper Perennial, 2008.

Marglin, Stephen A. *The Dismal Science: How Thinking Like an Economist Undermines Community.* Cambridge, MA: Harvard University Press, 2008.

McDonough, William, and Michael Braungart. *Cradle to Cradle: Remaking the Way We Make Things.* New York: North Point, 2002.

Meadows, Donella, Jorgen Randers, and Dennis L. Meadows. *Limits to Growth: The 30-Year Update.* White River Junction, VT: Chelsea Green, 2004.

Merchant, Caroline. *Reinventing Eden: The Fate of Nature in Western Culture.* New York: Routledge, 2003.

Merkel, Jim. *Radical Simplicity.* Gabriola Island, BC: New Society, 2003.

Meyer, Marvin, and Kurt Bergel. *Reverence for Life: The Ethics of Albert Schweitzer for the Twenty-First Century.* Syracuse, NY: Syracuse University Press, 2002.

Monbiot, George. *The Age of Consent: Manifesto for a New World Order.* London: Harper Perennial, 2003.

———. *Heat.* Toronto: Doubleday, 2006.

Nadeau, Robert L. *The Environmental Endgame: Mainstream Economics, Ecological Disaster, and Human Survival.* New Brunswick, NJ: Rutgers University Press, 2006.

Naylor, R. T. *Wages of Crime: Black Markets, Illegal Finance, and the Underworld Economy.* Ithaca, NY: Cornell University Press, 2002.

Nayyar, Deepak, ed. *Governing Globalization: Issues and Institutions.* Oxford: Oxford University Press, 2002.

Nelson, Melissa K. *Original Instructions: Indigenous Teachings for a Sustainable Future.* Rochester, VT: Bear, 2008.

Nelson, Robert H. *Economics as Religion: From Samuelson to Chicago and Beyond.* State College: Pennsylvania State University Press, 2001.

Nussbaum, Martha. *Frontiers of Justice.* Cambridge, MA: Harvard University Press, 2006.

Patomaki, Heikki. *Democratising Globalisation: The Leverage of the Tobin Tax.* London: Zed Books, 2001.

Perkins, John. *Confessions of an Economic Hit Man.* San Francisco: Berrett-Koehler, 2004.

Pimentel, David, Laura Westra, and Reed F. Noss, eds. *Ecological Integrity: Integrating Environment, Conservation, and Health.* Washington, DC: Island, 2002.

Polanyi, Karl. *The Great Transformation: The Political and Economic Origins of Our Time.* Boston: Beacon, 1957.

Ponting, Clive. *A Green History of the World.* New York: Penguin, 1991.

Powelson, John P. *The Moral Economy.* Ann Arbor: University of Michigan Press, 1998.

Punshon, John. *Portrait in Gray: A Short History of the Quakers.* London: Britain Yearly Meeting, 2006.

Reeves, Hubert and Frédéric Lenoir. *Mal de Terre.* Paris: Seuil, 2003.

Sachs, Wolfgang, and Tilman Santarius, eds. *Fair Future: Resource Conflicts, Security and Global Justice.* London: Zed Books, 2007.

Sandel, Michael. *Public Philosophy.* Cambridge, MA: Harvard University Press, 2005.

Saul, John Ralston. *The Collapse of Globalism and the Reinvention of the World.* Woodstock, NY: Overlook, 2005.

Schellnhuber, Hans Joachim, Paul J. Crutzen, William C. Clark, Martin Claussen, and Hermann Held, eds. *Earth System Analysis for Sustainability.* Cambridge, MA: MIT Press, 2004.

Schneider, Eric D., and Dorion Sagan. *Into the Cool: Energy Flow, Thermodynamics, and Life.* Chicago: University of Chicago Press, 2005.

Scholte, Jan Aart. *Globalization: A Critical Introduction.* 2nd ed. New York: Palgrave MacMillan, 2005.

Schrödinger, Erwin. *What Is Life?* Cambridge: Cambridge University Press, 1967.

Schweitzer, Albert. *Out of My Life and Thought.* New York: Henry Holt, 1933.

———. *The Philosophy of Civilization.* Amherst, NY: Prometheus Books, 1987.

Serres, Michel. *The Natural Contract.* Ann Arbor: University of Michigan Press, 1995.

Simms, Andrew. *Ecological Debt: The Health of the Planet and the Wealth of Nations.* London: Pluto, 2005.

Speth, James Gustave. *The Bridge at the Edge of the World: Capitalism, the Environment, and Crossing from Crisis to Sustainability.* New Haven, CT: Yale University Press, 2008.

———. *Red Sky at Morning: America and the Crisis of the Global Environment.* New Haven, CT: Yale University Press, 2004.

Speth, James Gustave, and Peter M. Haas. *Global Environmental Governance.* Washington, DC: Island, 2006.

Stiglitz, Joseph E. *Making Globalization Work.* New York: W. W. Norton, 2006.

Suzuki, David, and Holly Dressel. *Good News for a Change.* Toronto: Stoddart, 2002.

Sveiby, Karl-Erik, and Tex Skuthorpe. *Treading Lightly: The Hidden Wisdom of the World"s Oldest People.* Crows Nest, NSW: Allen and Unwin, 2006.

Tainter, Joseph. *The Collapse of Complex Societies.* Cambridge: Cambridge University Press, 1988.

Taylor, Paul. *Respect for Nature: A Theory of Environmental Ethics.* Princeton, NJ: Princeton University Press, 1986.

Thurow, Lester. "Income Distribution as a Pure Public Good." *Quarterly Journal of Economics* (1971): 327–36.

Van DeVeer, Donald, and Christine Pierce. *The Environmental Ethics and Policy Book: Philosophy, Ecology, Economics.* 3rd ed. Belmont, CA: Wadsworth, 2003.

Victor, Peter. *Managing Without Growth.* Cheltenham, UK: Edward Elgar, 2008.

Walker, Brian, and David Salt. *Resilience Thinking: Sustaining Ecosystems and People in a Changing World*. Washington, DC: Island, 2006.

Walvin, James. *The Quakers: Money and Morals*. London: John Murray, 1997.

Wilson, E. O. *The Creation: An Appeal to Save Life on Earth*. New York: W. W. Norton, 2006.

Wood, Ellen Meiksins. *The Origin of Capitalism: A Longer View*. London: Verso, 2002.

Woodbridge, Roy. *The Next World War: Tribes, Cities, Nations, and Ecological Decline*. Toronto: University of Toronto Press, 2004.

Acknowledgments

Right Relationship is inspired by the tradition of ecological economics. This body of thinking was originated in the twentieth century by such figures as Frederick Soddy, Nicholas Georgescu-Roegen, Herman Daly, and Robert Costanza. In this regard the writers of this book stand on the shoulders of giants. With due humility, we have endeavored to join their insights to a scientifically informed ethics, and to trace the implications of these points of view for the evolution of human institutions at this critical juncture in life's journey on the earth.

We also drew inspiration from Quakers who, in addition to Kenneth Boulding, laid important groundwork for the ideas in this book. Gilbert White, past president of Haverford College, a geographer, and a preeminent expert on managing water access conflicts, participated in the founding of the Quaker Institute for the Future. Walter Haines, another participant in the founding meetings of the QIF, has spoken from the experience of decades of teaching, research, and writing about the need for economics to change course. Morris Mitchell, who was the founding president of Friends World College, always sought to prepare students to become agents of social change on behalf of the commonwealth of life. Sam and Miriam Levering, and others at the Quaker United Nations Office, devoted a major part of their lives to creating and seeking international support for the Law of the Sea as a step toward global environmental governance. John P. Powelson, an economist, in 1998 published *The Moral Economy*, a book on how the economy should work for the benefit of all and especially for those in poverty.

Peter Brown would like to acknowledge the Edinburgh Studies in World Ethics, edited by Nigel Dower. Brown's own *Ethics, Economics and International Relations: Transparent Sovereignty in the Commonwealth of Life* appeared in this series and laid much of the intellectual groundwork that made the present work possible. It is published and distributed in North America by Black Rose Press under the title *The Commonwealth of Life: Economics For a Flourishing Earth*, second edition.

Two people were especially helpful in the writing of the book. First and foremost, thanks go to Leonard Joy, who brought decades of experience with international institutions and important insights on the need to focus on values development as a key to solving our current ethical and ecological crisis. Enormous thanks go, as well, to Holly Dressel, who shared her wisdom, substantive knowledge on the environment, and clear writing skill at several stages of the development of the book; this book would not be what it is without her.

Many people gave especially generously of their time and talents. They are: Mark Aneilski, Worth Bateman, Ed Dreby, Dianne Dumanoski, John Ehrenfeld, Myron Frankman, Newton Garver, Tom Head, Maria Ivanova, David Millar, Suzanne Moore, Cartter Patten, Matthias Ruth, Daniel Seeger, William Vitek, Stephen K. West, and Mick Womersley.

We are also grateful to others who helped with the development of this book: Peter Adams, Tom Allison, Bob Baden, Nick Bagnall, Mary Ellen Batiuk, Carlos Bernal, Marie-Helene Beaudry, Russell Brinsfield, Louis Bruneau, Philippe Buc, Julie Bukar, Wilfred Candler,

Wayne Cartwright, Pamela Chen, Amy Chester, Kendra Cipollini, Bicky Corman, Gray Cox, Herman Daly, Claudia de Windt, Linda Edgerly, Phil Emmi, Janine Ferretti, Jim Fitzsimmons, Derek Foote, Steve Galluccio, Cecily Garver, Julia Garver, Ted Garver, Émile Gaudreault, Mark Goldberg, David Goodin, Esmail Hejazifar, Laura Ward Holliday, John Howell, Helen Hughes, William V. Kennedy, Hollister Knowlton, Rick Kooperburg, Maggie Lawton, Tracy McCowen, Kai McGiver, Miriam McGiver, Anne Mitchell, Sabrina Morelli, Mark Myers, Byron Neuhaus, Patricia Nolan, Richard Norgaard, Katia Opalka, Rod Oram, Greg Pendleton, Ellie Perkins, Stephen Potthoff, Wendy Reid, Fabian Rüchardt, Carla Sbert, Lois Schiffer, Jeremy Schmidt, Deborah Scott, Grace Seybold, Michael Snarr, Robert S. Sprinkle, Shelley Tanenbaum, Joel Ann Todd, Jonathan Westeinde, Marta Wilkinson, Dorothy Williams, and Jack Woodward.

Finally, it would be impossible to overstate our exhilaration of working with Berrett-Koehler, our publisher. The reviews it commissioned from Douglas Dupler, Pamela J. Gordon, Jeanne Kahwajy, Ellyn Kerr, and Carol Metzker were excellent both on the merits of the argument and on their accessibility. Johanna Vondeling's constructive, visionary comments shaped the book and inspired us to new and, we hope, useful insights to help create a world that works for all.

Index

About the Moral Economy Project

THE QUAKER INSTITUTE FOR THE FUTURE (QIF) launched the Moral Economy Project in 2005 to address Friends' concerns about the human prospect in a world of unbridled growth and increasing ecological degradation. QIF seeks to help generate systematic insight, knowledge, and wisdom that can inform public policy in ways that will enable us all to live more fully in "the virtue of that life and power" that leads us to treat every human being, each community of life, and the whole earth as manifestations of the Divine. QIF aims to enhance Friends' understanding on issues of critical importance for the future of the earth's life communities, and to help bring this understanding into corporate witness and public discourse on public policy for the common good.

The vision of the Moral Economy Project (MEP) is that the global political-economic order shifts from one of unrestrained economic growth, ecological degradation, and social inequity to one that preserves and enhances social and ecological well-being. This is a vision of *right relationship with the commonwealth of life*. A key part of this vision is global and local governance that is grounded in a coherent ethical and scientific foundation and that fulfills key functions: a comprehensive understanding of the ecological limits on the human economy, a system to protect global commons, a set of global rules that maintain the economy within ecological limits, and an effective global system of enforcement and rule of law.

The MEP's mission is to engage in dialogue and action toward development and implementation of ideas for forms of governance needed to steer the global political and economic order toward right relationship with life's commonwealth.

The Quaker Institute for the Future sponsored, and was pleased to support, the team project that resulted in this volume. QIF saw the book's special merit in clearly identifying the great crisis of our time and offering principles to be applied in response. Its findings contribute to an ongoing dialogue process that needs to engage public policy professionals as well as a broad range of citizens. While the views expressed in this book are those of the authors, the work is endorsed by QIF's board of trustees, which is united in its sense of urgency about advancing dialogue toward prompt critical action needed to rectify the growing incoherence between the human economy and the integrity of the earth's ecological and social systems.

More information on the Moral Economy Project is available at www.moraleconomy.org.

About the Authors

PETER G. BROWN is a professor in the School of Environment, the Department of Geography, and the Department of Natural Resource Sciences at McGill University. Before going to McGill, he was Professor of Public Policy at the University of Maryland's graduate School of Public Affairs; while at Maryland he founded the Institute for Philosophy and Public Policy, and the School of Public Policy itself, and also established the School's Environmental Policy Programs. He is a graduate of Haverford College, and holds a master's degree in the philosophy of religion from Union Theological Seminary and Columbia University, and a Ph.D. from Columbia in philosophy. He is the author of *Restoring the Public Trust: A Fresh Vision for Progressive Government in America* (Beacon Press, 1994), and *Ethics, Economics and International Relations: Transparent Sovereignty in the Commonwealth of Life*, second edition (Edinburgh University Press, 2008); it is published in North America as *The Commonwealth of Life:*

Economics For a Flourishing Earth, second edition (Black Rose Books, 2008). He has edited and contributed to a number of other books and publications.

Brown is involved in conservation efforts in the James Bay and Southern regions of Quebec, as well as in Maryland. He operates tree farms in both locales and is a Certified Quebec Forest Producer, and in 1995 was Tree Farmer of the Year in Garrett County, Maryland. He is a member of the Religious Society of Friends.

Photo credit: Émile Gaudreault

GEOFFREY GARVER is an environmental consultant and lecturer in law in Montreal. From 2000 to 2007, he was a senior official at the North American Commission for Environmental Cooperation (www.cec.org), directing the unit that publishes detailed factual investigations of complaints by North American citizens that one of the NAFTA countries—Mexico, the United States, and Canada—is failing to effectively enforce its environmental law. At the CEC, he wrote reports on enforcement of laws on water pollution from Canadian pulp and paper mills, harm to fish habitat from logging in British Columbia, and the killing of migratory birds by timber harvesting in the United States. Previously, he spent nine years with the U.S. Justice Department's Environment and Natural Resources Division, first as a trial attorney and then as an acting assistant chief handling cases dealing with land and natural resource management, water rights, and environmental impact assessment. Some of his major cases concerned the Everglades' water quality, winter use and bison management in Yellowstone National Park, and water rights in Idaho and Oregon.

From 1993 to 1995, Garver was senior policy counsel in the Office of Enforcement and Compliance Assurance at the U.S. Environmental Protection Agency. Before joining the U.S. Justice Department in 1989, he was a judicial clerk for Judge Conrad Cyr in the federal district court in Bangor, Maine. He received a bachelor of science degree in chemical engineering from Cornell University in 1982 and a juris doctor degree, cum laude, from the University of Michigan Law School in 1987. At Michigan, he was an editor of the *Michigan Law Review*.

Garver grew up in a Quaker family in rural western New York.

KEITH HELMUTH has been primarily an entrepreneur, business manager, and community development activist. He is a founding board member of the Quaker Institute for the Future. Now living in Woodstock, New Brunswick, he spent the last ten years as manager of Penn Book Center, in Philadelphia. During the prior three decades he and his wife, Ellen, operated North Hill Farm in western New Brunswick. During that time they helped found the Woodstock Farm Market Cooperative and the Speerville Mill Cooperative. Keith Helmuth served on the Carleton Pioneer Credit Union board of directors for twenty-five years. During the 1970s he worked with the Public Participation Programmes of the Saint John Valley Regional Planning Commission and the Man and Resources Commission, Atlantic Region. From 1967 to 1970 he was on the faculty of Friends World College where he taught social ecology and environmental studies, served as director of library development, and was the founding chairperson of the Independent Studies Program. He spent a year at the college's East African Center as director of economic development and environmental studies.

Helmuth is a graduate of the State University of Iowa (in intellectual history, humanities, and East Asia studies). He is the author of two Canadian Quaker Pamphlets: *If John Woolman Were Among Us: Reflections on Flush Toilets and Motor Vehicles* and *From Arrowhead to Hand Axe: In Search of Ecological Guidance*, as well as a volume of poems for children, *Beauty Is the Earth's Bright Call*.

ROBERT HOWELL has many years of experience as a manager, consultant, and university teacher with competencies in strategic visioning, strategic planning, governance and policy setting, organizational and systems design, and implementation, as well as business ethics. He teaches business ethics at the School of Integrated Business, AUT University in Auckland, New Zealand, and is the CEO of the Council for Socially Responsible Investment New Zealand. He has worked in advisory, teaching, and CEO positions in the health, local authority, international education, and nonprofit sectors.

Howell has played a significant role in the introduction of social and environmental factors into New Zealand investment. He has assisted in introducing nonviolent conflict resolution training to the Indonesian police force. He has led and worked with Aotearoa New Zealand Friends to identify a strategic appreciation of climate change and its long-term social and economic consequences.

STEVE SZEGHI is a professor of economics at Wilmington College where he has taught for twenty years, been active in faculty governance, and served for many years as department head and area coordinator. He received his Ph.D in economics from the University of Cincinnati. Today his research focuses on themes of social justice, fair distribution, environmentalism, and concerns for indigenous cultural survival. In addition to being an academic, Szeghi has been active throughout his life in fighting for social justice and ecological balance. Beginning at the age of 15 through his mid-20s he worked with Cesar Chavez and the United Farm Workers. He continues to work with several labor unions, as well as American Indian tribal governments, cultural survival groups, and environmental organizations. He is currently developing several student study and research trip courses to the American Southwest where students study and research the interrelationships between wilderness, American Indian communities, and the cultural and environmental impacts of human activities in the Southwest.

About Berrett-Koehler Publishers

BERRETT-KOEHLER is an independent publisher dedicated to an ambitious mission: Creating a World That Works for All.

We believe that to truly create a better world, action is needed at all levels—individual, organizational, and societal. At the individual level, our publications help people align their lives with their values and with their aspirations for a better world. At the organizational level, our publications promote progressive leadership and management practices, socially responsible approaches to business, and humane and effective organizations. At the societal level, our publications advance social and economic justice, shared prosperity, sustainability, and new solutions to national and global issues.

A major theme of our publications is "Opening Up New Space." They challenge conventional thinking, introduce new ideas, and foster positive change. Their common quest is changing the underlying beliefs, mindsets, and structures that keep generating the same cycles of problems, no matter who our leaders are or what improvement programs we adopt.

We strive to practice what we preach—to operate our publishing company in line with the ideas in our books. At the core of our approach is *stewardship*, which we define as a deep sense of responsibility to administer the company for the benefit of all of our "stakeholder" groups: authors, customers, employees, investors, service providers, and the communities and environment around us.

We are grateful to the thousands of readers, authors, and other friends of the company who consider themselves to be part of the "BK Community." We hope that you, too, will join us in our mission.

A BK Currents Book

This book is part of our BK Currents series. BK Currents books advance social and economic justice by exploring the critical intersections between business and society. Offering a unique combination of thoughtful analysis and progressive alternatives, BK Currents books promote positive change at the national and global levels. To find out more, visit www.bkcurrents.com.

Be Connected

Visit Our Website   Go to www.bkconnection.com to read exclusive previews and excerpts of new books, find detailed information on all Berrett-Koehler titles and authors, browse subject-area libraries of books, and get special discounts.

Subscribe to Our Free E-Newsletter   Be the first to hear about new publications, special discount offers, exclusive articles, news about bestsellers, and more! Get on the list for our free e-newsletter by going to www.bkconnection.com.

Get Quantity Discounts   Berrett-Koehler books are available at quantity discounts for orders of ten or more copies. Please call us toll-free at (800) 929-2929 or email us at bkp.orders@aidcvt.com.

Host a Reading Group   For tips on how to form and carry on a book reading group in your workplace or community, see our website at www.bkconnection.com.

Join the BK Community   Thousands of readers of our books have become part of the "BK Community" by participating in events featuring our authors, reviewing draft manuscripts of forthcoming books, spreading the word about their favorite books, and supporting our publishing program in other ways. If you would like to join the BK Community, please contact us at bkcommunity@bkpub.com.